Bacon & Eggs
the cookbook

Global Publishing Group
Australia • New Zealand • Singapore • America • London

Bacon & Eggs
the cookbook

Foreword by Chef Tom Rutherford

Monique Lambert

DISCLAIMER

All the information, techniques, skills and concepts contained within this publication are of the nature of general comment only and are not in any way recommended as individual advice. The intent is to offer a variety of information to provide a wider range of choices now and in the future, recognising that we all have widely diverse circumstances and viewpoints. Should any reader choose to make use of the information contained herein, this is their decision, and the contributors (and their companies), authors and publishers do not assume any responsibilities whatsoever under any condition or circumstances. It is recommended that the reader obtain their own independent advice.

First Edition 2017

Copyright © 2017 Monique Lambert

Recipes, Design, Photography and Styling, Monique Lambert

All rights are reserved. The material contained within this book is protected by copyright law, no part may be copied, reproduced, presented, stored, communicated or transmitted in any form by any means without prior written permission.

National Library of Australia

Cataloguing-in-Publication entry:

Creator: Lambert, Monique Nicole, author

Title: Bacon & Eggs: The Cookbook / Monique Lambert.

ISBN: 9781925288469 (paperback)

Subjects: Cooking (Bacon)
Cooking (Eggs)
Cookbooks.

Published by Global Publishing Group
PO Box 517 Mt Evelyn, Victoria 3796 Australia
Email info@GlobalPublishingGroup.com.au

For further information about orders:
Phone: +61 3 9726 4133 or Fax +61 3 8648 6871

This book is dedicated to my A-Team, without whom, this book would never have been.

Jessica Thorne, Loan Mas, Monica Cook, Margot Davies, Nadine Welke,
Johanna 'Swifty' Airlie, Roly Stokes, Maria Stanford, Rosalinda Knochelle,
Brooke Duncan, Lisa Taylor, Liz Allnutt, Simone Bedford, Tara Kleiner,
Christina Panagiotopoulos, Rachael Von Pein, Craig O'Donnell, Nicole Roma,
Lauren Sewell, Nicki Stepan, Ben Moyle, Simone Weller, Carly Sandilands, Jason Baumber,
Khanh Trieu, John Logiacco, Danny Stefanovski, Jason Cram,
Amanda Moore, Martin Van Der Horst, and all the other dedicated taste testers at the
Australian international motor shows.

Acknowledgements

One of the best things about writing this book has been the incredible support along the way. It has been a tremendous, unexpected journey in writing and photographing this book. As with any major project, there are always very special people along the way, who from the shadows, greatly contributed to making this book happen, so I'd like to take the opportunity to thank you all.

During the time of writing this book, I have seen the growth of the food industry. And with it came the new age of modern chefs, many of whom have embraced modern day cooking, motivating domestic cooks worldwide, and most importantly, inspiring me to reinvent old to new. The likes of Jamie Oliver, Heston Blumenthal, Marco Pierre White, Ainsley Harriott, Colin Fassnidge and George Calombaris have been just that for me, inspirational.

To my mentors, Darren Stephens and Kelly Mayne from Global Publishing Group, and Rachael Birmingham, co-founder of *4 Ingredients*; your unwavering support and guidance has been incredible and truly appreciated.

As a house mother for many years, looking after international students, I took it upon myself to experiment with other cuisines from around the globe. My dear students, and most importantly Felix and Kai, your 'thumbs' up or 'thumbs down' policy provided me with extended patience in the long run. Thank you for your honesty and patience until I got it right!

To my wonderful friends that have sent me tips and photos they've seen here and there (in thought that I may not have seen things that could possibly enhance my book), thank you for thinking of me and for caring enough to do this.

Last but certainly not least, there are three very special friends that I wish to acknowledge for their constant reassurance. Three lifelong friends whom with every wall I hit, or hurdle I thought was too high to overcome, they peeled me off the pavement and slapped me with warm words of wisdom and perseverance. You cushioned the blows with faith and encouragement, and for this I am forever grateful. Karen List, Lindy Green and Karen Colpitts, thank you for just being you, and always being there for me.

FREE BONUS RECIPES

Thank you for buying **Bacon & Eggs**!

As a special gift just for you, I would like to give you **3 FREE bonus recipes**, exclusive to **Bacon & Eggs** readers.

Go to **www.MoniqueLambert.com.au**
and register to receive your FREE downloadable recipes.

There are also loads of extra goodies on my website, just for you.

To gain instant access to these FREE resources, simply visit this website:

www.MoniqueLambert.com.au

Contents

Foreword 1
About this cookbook 3

Breakfast   5

Poached Eggs with Chorizo Ratatouille 6
Bacon Soldiers & Soft Boiled Eggs 8
Bubble & Squeal 10
Green Eggs & Ham 12
Panini Bruschetta with Poached Eggs & Bacon 14
Classic Fry-Up 16
Egg White Omelette with Tomato & Bacon Salsa 18
Roasted Brussel Sprouts & Hazelnut Omelette 20
Eggs Foo Yung (Chinese Omelette) 22
Croissant Croque Madam 24

Brunch & Anytime Snacks   27

Crumbed Salt & Pepper Yolks 28
Gehakte Leber in a Blanket (Chopped Liver) 30
Peking Porky 32
Asparagus, Prosciutto & Eggs Mimosa 34
Eggs Kilpatrick 36
Devilled Eggs Kilpatrick 36
Scotch Eggs 38
Ham & Mushroom Crepes 40
Ricotta & Bacon Hotcakes 42
Little Pork Balls with Coriander & Lime Dipping Sauce 44
Omelette Sang Choy Bow 46

Salads   49

Pink Salad with Mascarpone & Cumin Dressing 50
Caesar Salad Fresh Spring Rolls 52
BLT in a Bowl 54
Potato Salad with Bacon & Egg 56
Succotash Salad 58
Israeli Salad & Boiled Eggs 60

Noodles / Pasta / Rice   63

Californian Rolls with BBQ Pork & Egg Salad 64
Singapore Noodles with Pork & Egg Threads 66
Pearl Couscous Carbonara 68
Risotto with Pancetta, Bacon & Poached Eggs 70
Kedgeree 72

Breads   75

Bacon & Egg Cupcakes 76
Spicy Salami & Bacon Bread 78
Florentine Brunch Baguettes 80

Soups   83

Congee (Chinese Rice Soup) 84
Stracciatella 86
Salmorejo 88
Smokey Bacon Stock 90
Bacon & Egg Soup 92

Quiches, Pies & Tarts — 95

Quiche Lorraine 96
Bacon, Feta & Egg Tart 98
Garlic Baguette & Butter Pudding 100

Mains — 103

Frittata with Bacon & Peas 104
Sticky Pork Spare Ribs 106
Pork Schnitzels with Sauce Gribiche & Rainbow Slaw 108
Greek Baked Pork Chops – Alonissos style 110
Russian Cabbage Rolls 112
Spanakopita (Spinach, Feta & Bacon Pie) 114
'No Bun' Gourmet Burgers with Beetroot Cream 116

Chook's Pantry — 119

Onion Confit 120
Chicken Stock 122
Slow Roasted Tomatoes 124
Home-Made Tomato Passata 126
Creamed Spinach 128
Minced Onion, Minced Ginger & Minced Garlic 130
Béchamel (White) Sauce 131

About the author 133

Foreword

Tom Rutherford is a renowned chef, entrepreneur and industry leader in Australian catering and corporate events. Spanning 35 years, his illustrious career was launched at Le Gavroche, a three Michelin star restaurant in London, where he honed his craft under the expert tutelage of Albert Roux himself.

At a time when catering wasn't considered a 'proper job for a chef' he made the leap from chef to catering entrepreneur. In 1987, he founded Truffle Group Catering Company, through which he pioneered the catering industry for over 20 years with his restaurant quality food and creative flair. Tom was chosen to produce never-before-seen food for the prestigious Cointreau Balls and Australian launch events for Louis Vuitton, Chanel and Hermés to name a few.

Tom's strategic mission, to effectively create a professional Australian catering events industry, has always been his driving force. In the 1980s catering was confined to the predictable formula of 'dim sums and sausage rolls'; lacking style, quality and innovation. However, Tom's vision and work through the Truffle Group changed all that.

In acknowledging Tom's contribution, famous chef Tetsuya Wakuda says: "I consider Tom to be a pioneer of the catering industry, changing the way we eat at all manner of events."

"What I love about this book, is that Monique really has considered the culture of breakfast and highlighted the trend of the "all-day Breakie" menu, she has created many inspirational takes on the classics, carefully considered the diverse Asian and European cultures to create many inventive and delicious dishes easy and quick to prepare and serve

With so many takes on the humble bacon and egg any cook can find a recipe to suit any time of day, flavour or diet preference, from simple to more the complex recipes. From soups, salads, snacks and meals with a smattering of old favourites and many moreish new creations.

The recipes are well thought through, unique and deliciously photographed. Monique's recipes can be easily adapted, with vegetarianism on the rise they are easy to adjust to your desire.

This book is on trend, innovative and imaginative allowing easy personal touches to be made, I am sure it will be a regular "go to" for any enthusiastic cook and great addition to any collection."

Tom

About this cookbook

I really look forward to going out for breakfast and I can't think of anything more enticing to the palate than a hearty bacon and eggs breakfast. In my opinion, there's no meal as good as a plate of crispy bacon, perfectly poached eggs, hot toast with real butter with a side of garlic mushrooms and sautéed spinach – absolute heaven!

To many people around the world Bacon and Eggs is what pasta is to Italians, bagels to the New Yorkers, haggis to the Scottish and sashimi to the Japanese. Almost like a culture in itself.

This book contains recipes using both eggs and pork, and other porcine bi-products, such as ham, prosciutto, sausages, and of course the star attraction – bacon. Many recipes are traditional, although I have prepared them in my own special way, with little tweaks and personal touches, which I believe are creatively unique and deliciously irresistible. There are no rules to adhere to regarding the lists of ingredients I have provided. You can create your own versions of my adaptations and most recipes provide various alternatives for non-meat eaters.

Both individually and combined, bacon and eggs are incredibly versatile. In this book, I will show you how to create fabulous recipes that can be eaten any time of the day.

Don't be fooled by the title – this book is not just about breakfast. There are hundreds of possible combinations to create fabulous meals using any of the featured ingredients. Here are just a few.

I hope you enjoy this book as much as I have enjoyed cooking, tasting and selecting the recipes for you.

Breakfast

Breakfast

Poached Eggs with Chorizo Ratatouille

It wasn't until recently that poached eggs jumped to the top of my favourites list. After several attempts to make the perfect poached egg, I started tasting and enjoying my 'flops'. They all tasted great, it just took me over 100 attempts to perfect the cooking technique. Served with a delicious chorizo and vegetable ratatouille, the flavours are beautifully complimented, and make a lovely light meal.

Ingredients – serves 2

2 tablespoons olive oil
1 **chorizo** sausage, finely diced
1 large garlic clove, minced
½ Spanish onion, finely diced
1 small eggplant, finely diced (optional)
2 medium Roma tomatoes, skins and seeds removed, finely diced
1 tablespoon tomato paste
1 medium celery rib, finely diced
1 medium zucchini, finely diced
Pinch of sea salt (optional)
4 poached **eggs**, for serving

Method

Chorizo Ratatouille:

In a medium saucepan, heat the olive oil over medium - high heat. Add the chorizo and cook for 3 minutes, or until browned and the fragrant oils are released. Add the onions, garlic and eggplant, if using. Cook for a further 5 minutes before adding the tomatoes, tomato paste and celery. Stir gently for 5 minutes before finally adding the zucchini. Season with salt and cook for another 3 - 4 minutes or until all the vegetables have softened. Arrange eggs on the plates and top with chorizo ratatouille. Serve immediately.

CHOOK'S TIPS

Make sure you have all your preparation done before you start. Chicken, bacon or wurst can be substituted for the chorizo. I've added just a pinch of salt here, as some chorizo sausages can be quite salty, so check the seasoning as you go. Vegetarians can adapt this dish by leaving out the chorizo. You can also use fresh chilli placed in the frying pan in the initial stage with the chorizo - it really packs a punch. If you don't like it too hot and do like a little spice, try a dash of Worcestershire sauce. Another great idea: chorizo ratatouille is fabulous as a jacket potato (baked potato) filling, or stirred through some mashed potato, or even tossed through your favourite pasta.

Breakfast

Bacon Soldiers & Soft Boiled Eggs

We all know Soldier Toasties in their various forms and here's a delightful twist using bacon and coriander butter. This flavour came about accidentally. A few coriander sprigs snuck in as I grabbed a handful of parsley. I only realised after I had processed the ingredients in the mini whiz, and caught that unmistakable scent of fresh coriander. Good thing I didn't discard the batch because it turned out great. This Bacon & Eggs family favourite is sure to be a winner in your house.

Ingredients – serves 2

4 large fresh **eggs**, room temperature
4 slices white bread, crusts trimmed
4 rindless short-cut **bacon** rashers
½ tablespoon parsley, finely chopped
1 tablespoon coriander, finely chopped (optional)
1 - 2 tablespoons butter, softened

Method

Preheat the oven to 180°C. Line a baking sheet with baking paper. Place bacon in a small food processor and with short bursts, process the bacon until finely minced. In a small bowl, combine the minced bacon with softened butter, parsley and coriander, if using. Liberally butter each bread slice with the bacon butter. Cut each slice of bread into 3 even sized fingers. Bake for 8 - 10 minutes or until toast is golden brown and bacon is cooked. Meanwhile, place eggs in a small pot of water and bring to the boil. Cook for 3 - 4 minutes for soft-boiled eggs. Stir the water constantly so the yolks are centered. Serve immediately with the bacon soldier toasties.

 CHOOK'S TIPS

My nieces and nephews just love these fingers. I've also made them a peanut butter and bacon version and it worked a treat.

www.MoniqueLambert.com.au

Breakfast

Bubble & Squeal

Bubble and Squeal is such a fun breakfast or brunch meal. The traditional recipe, called Bubble & Squeak, is made from leftover meat and vegetables, usually corned beef, potatoes and cabbage and fried up into little patties. I've created a really cute dish without cabbage and corned beef, and simply added a few freezer standbys. No surprise, the corned beef has been substituted with bacon.

Ingredients – makes 6-8 patties

500g potatoes, cooked and peeled

200g diced **bacon,** cooked and drained

1 large fresh **egg** plus 2 fresh **egg yolks**

1 tablespoon parsley, finely chopped

150g mixed diced vegetables (carrots, peas and corn kernels), par-boiled for 3 minutes

2 tablespoons minced onion or 1 tablespoon prepared onion confit (cooked, caramelised onion)

Sea salt and freshly ground black pepper

Olive oil for shallow frying, or you can use half butter and half oil

4 fresh **eggs**, for serving

Method

In a medium bowl, mash the potatoes and add the bacon, egg and yolks, parsley, vegetables and onion or onion confit, if using. Season to taste and gently mix until well combined. In a large non-stick frying pan, heat 1 tablespoon of oil, or half oil and butter, over medium heat. Carefully place 1/3 cup prepared mixture into the frying pan, and repeat to make 4 patties, allowing room for spreading. Reduce the heat to low and cook the patties for approximately 4 - 5 minutes on one side, or until browned and crispy underneath. Using two spatulas, carefully turn each patty, and cook for a further 4 minutes or until browned and crispy. Repeat with remaining mixture, using a little more oil and butter if needed. Cover, set aside and keep warm. Cook the eggs as you like them and serve an egg on top of each Bubble & Squeal patty.

CHOOK'S TIPS

I've used egg rings for a neater presentation. If you use egg rings, lightly butter the inside of 4 x 7cm diameter rings and place them in the frying pan. Pack the mixture in well, leaving no 'air pockets'. Use tongs when handling the egg rings. Keep the patties small, as they tend to break up if they are too large. The vegetarian option is to leave out the bacon and add some sun-dried tomatoes and grilled, chopped capsicum to the potato mixture.

Breakfast

Green Eggs & Ham

Inspired by Dr Seuss, this Green Eggs, Peas and Ham version is a little more grown up and very different to what the good doctor had in mind - lightly browned ham off the bone and softly scrambled, piquant eggs nesting in flakey, hot, buttery pastry cases. A few little stages to follow, but the final presentation is colourful, novel and really, really tasty.

Ingredients – serves 4 for a large meal or 8 for entrée

8 vol au vent cases, 10cm diameter
2 tablespoons butter, melted
400g leg **ham**
1 tablespoon olive oil
1 medium brown onion, finely chopped or
1 tablespoon prepared onion confit (cooked, caramelised onion)
½ teaspoon garlic, minced
8 large fresh **eggs**
80ml thickened cream
1 tablespoon tiny capers
2 tablespoons parsley, finely chopped
2 tablespoons pesto
2 spring onions, finely sliced, reserving a small amount of green tips for garnish
1 cup frozen peas, cooked and cooled, reserving a few plump ones for garnish

CHOOK'S TIPS

You can use sausages, bacon, prosciutto, or even leftover barbecue chicken as an alternative to the ham. And for the vegetarians, can the ham!! You'll be just as happy with these eggs served on their own in the vol au vents. As an alternative to the vol au vents, Green Egg scramble is great on toast or as a filling for jacket potatoes (baked potatoes) too.

Method

Preheat the oven to 180°C. Arrange the vol au vent cases on a lined tray, brush with butter and bake for 18 – 20 minutes or until golden brown. In the meantime, brown the ham on both sides in a large frying pan over medium heat. Remove the ham from the pan, cover, set aside, and keep warm. In the same frying pan, add the olive oil and onions, and cook over medium heat until the onions are soft, fragrant and translucent, about 5 minutes. Turn the heat to low, add the garlic and cook for a further minute, stirring every so often. If using onion confit, add the onion confit to the frying pan to gently warm, then add the garlic and cook for a minute or so until fragrant. Set aside to cool and wipe the frying pan clean. In a medium bowl, whisk the eggs and cream.

Add the onion-garlic confit, capers, parsley, pesto, spring onions and peas.

Heat the oil in the frying pan over medium - high heat and add the 'green eggs'. Immediately turn the heat to low. Using a wooden spoon, stir the eggs continuously in small circular motions so the eggs don't set like an omelette. When soft curds start to form, after approximately 1½ - 2 minutes, turn off the heat completely and continue stirring the eggs; they will continue to cook with residual heat from the frying pan. To serve, place the warmed vol au vents onto serving plates. Spoon the 'green eggs' into the vol au vent pastry cases, top with some ham, garnish with extra spring onions and peas and serve immediately.

www.MoniqueLambert.com.au

Breakfast

Panini Bruschetta with Poached Eggs & Bacon

I really enjoy eggs in the morning. In fact, I can eat eggs at any time of the day. This bruschetta makes a great breakfast, brunch or any time snack. Be sure to use a robust sourdough loaf or panini for this recipe.

Ingredients – serves 2

2 large portobello mushrooms, thickly sliced
2 sprigs of fresh thyme
Olive oil or butter for basting (optional)
1/3 cup chicken or vegetable stock
Sea salt and freshly ground black pepper
4 rindless short-cut **bacon** rashers
4 large fresh **eggs**
2 panini loaves, halved lengthways to make 4 slices
Extra thyme leaves, picked, for garnish

CHOOK'S TIPS

Additional poaching tips: When you place the eggs into the water, bring the dish as close to the water as possible. Once you've dropped the eggs into the water, leave them to set without stirring the water again, as the egg yolks could separate completely from the egg whites. I tend to poach only 1 egg at a time.

If you are making many poached eggs, they can be made in advance. Have a large shallow dish ready with iced water and follow the cooking steps. Place cooked eggs into iced water which will stop the cooking process. To reheat, just before serving drain the cold water and gently pour some boiling water around the eggs in the dish.

Thyme, rosemary, garlic or parsley can be used to add flavour to the mushrooms whilst baking. For a vegetarian alternative, omit the bacon and substitute with slow roasted Roma tomatoes, zucchinis or squash. Mushrooms can also be sliced and pan fried in a little butter and olive oil instead of baking.

Method

Mushrooms:

Preheat the oven to 180°C. Place the mushrooms in a medium baking dish. Baste with olive oil or butter, if using, and add stock, thyme, and season to taste. Cover loosely with foil and bake for 20 minutes or until soft and juicy.

Bacon:

Heat 1 teaspoon of olive oil in a large frying pan and cook the bacon over medium - high heat until browned on both sides. Cover, set aside, and keep warm.

Poached Eggs:

Half fill a large, deep saucepan with water and bring to a simmering boil, with minimal water movement. Break an egg into a small dish or saucer. Give the water a stir to create a whirlpool and carefully tip the egg into the water. Cook for approximately 3 minutes for runny yolks and 4 minutes for a slightly firmer yolk. Remove with slotted spoon, drain well on paper towels and set aside. Repeat with remaining eggs. To serve, place panini toast onto serving plates, remove mushrooms from the baking dish and place straight onto the toast. Top with bacon and poached eggs and any remaining baking juices, garnish with extra thyme leaves and serve immediately.

Breakfast

Classic Fry-Up

The dish of all breakfast dishes – the one you wake up dreaming about on a Sunday morning, the one that makes your tummy rumble in anticipation of – the classic fry up. Breakfast, lunch or dinner –2, 4, 6, 8 – can't wait!

Ingredients – serves 2

1 teaspoon butter
1 tablespoon olive oil
1 cup small button mushrooms
½ teaspoon garlic, minced
2 teaspoons fresh chives or parsley, finely chopped
Sea salt and freshly ground black pepper
1 medium brown onion, finely grated or 1 tablespoon prepared onion confit (cooked, caramelised onion)
1 cup cherry tomatoes
4 rindless **bacon** rashers
4 large fresh **eggs**
Rocket or baby spinach leaves, for garnish

CHOOK'S TIPS

Mushrooms and tomato salsa can be prepared in advance. Reheat in small saucepans or in a microwave, if preferred. For really big appetites, cook up a few chipolata sausages alongside the bacon. Vegetarians, are you sure you don't want to try this one?

Method

Mushrooms:

Heat the butter and 1 teaspoon of the oil in a small saucepan over medium heat and add the mushrooms, garlic, chives or parsley and season. Stir for 3 minutes until mushrooms are golden brown and juicy. Cover, set aside and keep warm.

Tomato Salsa:

Heat 2 teaspoons of the oil in another small saucepan over medium heat. Add the onion, season with a pinch of salt and stir for 5 minutes. Reduce the heat to low and continue cooking for a further 10 minutes until onions become translucent and caramelised, stirring every so often. Add the cherry tomatoes and cook for a further 3 minutes or until tomatoes start to blister and soften. If using onion confit, add the onion mixture to the saucepan to warm, then add tomatoes and cook for 3 minutes or until they start to blister. Cover, set aside and keep warm. Meanwhile, prepare the bacon.

Bacon:

Heat a teaspoon of olive oil in a frying pan and cook the bacon until browned on both sides. Drain, cover with foil and set aside.

Eggs:

Cook the eggs as you like them; fried, poached or scrambled. To serve, gently reheat the mushrooms and tomatoes. Arrange all ingredients onto serving plates, garnish with rocket or spinach and serve with crusty toast.

Breakfast

Egg White Omelette with Tomato & Bacon Salsa

If you're not a fan of egg yolks, then this is the breakfast for you. I love an egg white omelette. They're often served in hotels as part of the menu, and most restaurants and cafes will cook you up an egg white omelette upon request. Packed full of protein, this meal is a great start to the day.

Ingredients – serves 1

3 large fresh **egg whites**, (reserve yolks for another use)
2 teaspoons fresh chives, finely chopped
1 tablespoon parmesan cheese, finely grated (optional)
1 teaspoon light olive oil
Additional chives, uncut, for garnish
Sea salt

Bacon & Tomato Salsa

1 teaspoon olive oil
2 rindless **bacon** rashers, coarsely chopped
1 small brown onion, finely chopped
2 large Roma tomatoes, chopped, or 1 cup tinned crushed tomatoes
Sea salt and freshly ground black pepper

Method

Salsa:

Heat the oil in a small saucepan over medium heat. Add the onion and bacon and cook until onion is translucent and bacon is cooked through. Add the tomatoes, pepper and salt to season, and cook for 10 minutes or until tomatoes have softened and flavours have developed. Cover, set aside, and keep warm.

Omelette:

Combine the egg whites, chives, salt and parmesan cheese, if using. In a medium frying pan heat the oil over medium heat. Add the eggs and allow the omelette to set. Turn the heat down to low and gently tilt the pan, allowing the uncooked egg to run underneath the cooked egg. When the egg is set underneath and almost cooked on top, turn the heat off, as the omelette will continue to cook with residual heat from the frying pan. Garnish with fresh chives and serve immediately with warmed bacon and tomato salsa.

CHOOK'S TIPS

Remaining egg yolks can be frozen in airtight containers. Spring onions can replace the chives in this recipe for delicious flavour variations. Cooked chicken also works well instead of the bacon, or you can leave the meats out altogether for an easy, delectable vegetarian meal.

Breakfast

Roasted Brussel Sprouts & Hazelnut Omelette

Brussel sprouts — you either love them or loathe them. I happen to think they're sensational, so I use this winter favourite whenever I have a craving. Bacon, Brussel sprouts and hazelnuts work particularly well, so I've made this omelette for you to try — it really is delicious.

Ingredients - serves 2

8 Brussel sprouts
2 tablespoons olive oil
Sea salt and freshly ground black pepper
4 rindless **bacon** rashers, chopped into 2cm pieces
5 large fresh **eggs**
2 tablespoons thickened cream
½ cup roasted hazelnuts, coarsely chopped
Additional chopped roasted hazelnuts, for garnish

CHOOK'S TIPS

For a vegetarian version, just leave out the bacon (if you must) and serve with fried potatoes or slow-roasted tomatoes - just as dee-lish.

Method

Brussel sprouts:

Preheat the oven to 170°C. Cut the sprouts into quarters and place into a small roasting tray. Toss with 1 tablespoon of oil and a little salt. Roast the sprouts for 30 minutes, turning once after 15 minutes, until softened and outer leaves are crunchy. Remove from oven and set aside in the tray. Meanwhile, heat 1 teaspoon of the oil in a large frying pan and cook the bacon until browned on both sides. Drain and set aside to cool. Wipe the frying pan clean with paper towels.

Omelette:

Combine the eggs, cream, bacon and pepper. Heat 1 teaspoon of oil in a frying pan over medium heat. Add the eggs and allow the omelette to set. Turn the heat down to low and gently tilt the pan, allowing the uncooked egg to run underneath the cooked egg. Scatter the Brussel sprouts and ½ cup of chopped hazelnuts over the omelette. When the egg is set underneath and almost cooked on top, turn the heat off, as the omelette will continue to cook with residual heat from the frying pan. Carefully lift one half of the omelette to cover the other half and slide onto the serving plate. Garnish with remaining hazelnuts and serve immediately.

Breakfast

Eggs Foo Yung (Chinese Omelette)

There are many versions of this delicious Asian omelette. You can keep it really simple with just a few ingredients or turn it into a main meal by adding chicken, prawns or BBQ pork, or a combination of all three. This omelette is easily adapted to a vegetarian meal by using lots of extra fresh vegetables.

Ingredients – serves 2

1 tablespoon peanut oil or vegetable oil

¼ cup Asian shallots, finely chopped

1 large clove garlic, minced

1 tablespoon Japanese soy, or more, depending on taste

½ cup celery, thinly sliced

6 fresh shiitake mushrooms, finely sliced

1½ cups char siu barbecue **pork**, chopped to 1cm cubes

1 tablespoon oyster sauce, or more, depending on taste

½ teaspoon sesame oil

½ cup spring onions, sliced on the diagonal, reserving a few green tips for garnish

½ cup tinned bamboo shoots, rinsed, finely sliced lengthways

1 cup snow peas, sliced on the diagonal

1 cup baby spinach leaves (optional)

5 large fresh **eggs**

2 teaspoon fish sauce

1 cup bean sprouts, or snow peas, or spring onions, sliced thinly on the diagonal, for garnish

Char Siu Sauce

2 tablespoons char siu sauce

½ tablespoon light soy

1½ tablespoons corn flour

1 cup chicken stock

Method

Sauce:

Combine the soy, corn flour, prepared char siu sauce and chicken stock in a small saucepan over low - medium heat and cook until thick and glossy, approximately 2 minutes. Cover and keep warm.

Filling:

In a medium saucepan, heat half the oil over medium - high heat and cook the shallots and garlic until fragrant and translucent. Add the soy, celery, shiitake mushrooms, barbecue pork, oyster sauce, sesame oil, spring onions, and bamboo shoots. Gently stir to combine and cook for approximately 3 minutes. Turn heat down to low and add the snow peas and the spinach, if using, and continue cooking for another minute. Cover, set aside and keep warm.

Omelette:

Combine the fish sauce and the eggs. Heat half the remaining oil in a large frying pan over medium heat. Add the eggs and allow the omelette to set. Turn the heat down to low and gently tilt the pan, allowing the uncooked egg to run underneath the cooked egg. When the egg is set underneath and almost cooked on top, turn the heat off, as the omelette will continue to cook with residual heat from the frying pan. Place the omelette onto a serving plate. Add 1 cup of prepared barbecue pork filling to the centre of the omelette and enclose. Repeat for the second omelette. Garnish with a generous drizzle of warmed char siu sauce and bean sprouts, snow pea slices, or spring onions. Serve immediately.

CHOOK'S TIPS

For the delicious vegetarian version, leave out the barbecue pork and add grated carrots and steamed baby bok choy. For a main meal, I serve this omelette with steamed rice. Char siu sauce is available in Asian grocers.

Breakfast

Croissant Croque Madam

This is a classic French ham and cheese sandwich with an indulgent makeover. The original is a ham and cheese fried toastie topped with a béchamel sauce and then grilled. It's called a 'Croque Monsieur' at this stage, although when you add the egg, it becomes a 'Croque Madam'. Croissants are rich and buttery in their own right, so I've simply baked this one instead of frying it in any extra butter.

Ingredients – serves 1

1 croissant or 2 mini croissants
½ teaspoon Dijon mustard, or hot English mustard if preferred
2 thin slices leg **ham**
1½ tablespoons gruyere or other tasty cheese, grated
2 tablespoons prepared white sauce
1 teaspoon olive oil
1 large fresh **egg**

Method

Preheat the oven to 180°C. Line a baking tray with baking paper. Cut the croissants in half horizontally and place onto the tray. Butter the cut side of the croissant with the mustard. Top with the ham and cover with the lid of the croissant. Bake the croissant for 5 - 6 minutes or until crispy. Meanwhile, combine the white sauce and cheese and warm gently in a small saucepan. Remove the croissant from the oven and turn the griller on to high. Spread the cheesy white sauce over the top of the croissant and grill for 2 minutes or until melted and bubbling. Meanwhile, heat the oil in a small frying pan and cook the egg to your liking. Place the croissant on a serving plate, topped with the egg and bon appetite.

CHOOK'S TIPS

Try preparing this with a few slices of tomato in the croissant before baking, or serve with roasted tomatoes or some sautéed spinach on the side. Tomato and spinach will cut through the richness of the buttery croissant. As an alternative to the white sauce and grated cheese, you could use a store bought cheese sauce and pour over the top of the baked ham croissant - decadent and very delicious.

Brunch & Anytime Snacks

Brunch & Anytime Snacks

Crumbed Salt & Pepper Yolks

I love a good salt and pepper dish – fish, prawns, calamari and chicken – all the usual suspects. So, I thought I'd have a play with some yolks, and they turned out amazing. It's a very delicate operation, so you'll need to be patient, or there may be a few casualties along the way.

Ingredients – serves 2-3 as a snack

6 large fresh **eggs**

2 cups plain flour, for coating

2 additional **eggs**, beaten

2 cups fine bread crumbs, for coating

1 cup finely grated parmesan cheese

Freshly ground Szechuan pepper and sea salt, approximately 2 tablespoons each

Vegetable oil, for deep frying

Crackers for serving

Gehakte Leber (chopped liver) for serving – see next recipe

Method

Place the flour and beaten eggs in 2 separate medium size bowls. Mix the bread crumbs and parmesan in a large shallow dish and season well with the salt and pepper. Crack one egg and allow the white to run into a bowl, keeping the yolk in half the shell. Gently place the yolk into one hand and allow any remaining egg white to run through your fingers into the bowl. Holding the yolk in the 'wet' hand, delicately coat it in the flour, and use the other 'dry' hand to assist sprinkling the flour over the yolk until it's completely covered. Submerge yolks into the beaten eggs with the wet hand. Lift yolk up, allowing any excess egg wash to run between your fingers, then gently slip the coated yolk into the crumbing mix and with the dry hand, cover it completely with the crumbs. You can repeat this process again with egg wash and crumbs for a thicker coating if you like.

Make a few small wells in one corner of the crumbing mix. Gently rest each crumbed yolk in a well whilst preparing the next yolk. Heat the oil in a small deep saucepan over medium - high heat. When the oil is hot enough to turn a cube of bread brown in 30 seconds, gently lift the crumbed yolks and lower them into the oil. Use a wooden spoon to gently turn the yolks in the oil so they cook evenly. Cook for 1 – 1½ minutes or until golden and crunchy. The yolks will be runny. Remove with slotted spoon and drain on paper towels. Repeat process until all the eggs have been cooked. Serve with crackers and Gehakte Leber.

CHOOK'S TIPS

It's important to have all your ingredients ready in bowls before you start. This is a delicate operation and could get a bit messy, so remember to keep one hand for the 'wet' and one for the 'dry' ingredients and it will be so much easier. Remaining egg whites can be frozen in airtight containers. For an alternative flavour sensation, try using some chilli powder to the crumbing mix, then garnish with some sliced spring onions, chopped coriander and green chilli slices. If you happen to break any yolks along the way, add them to the egg wash. If you break too many yolks, make an omelette.

Brunch & Anytime Snacks

Gehakte Leber in a Blanket (Chopped Liver)

My good friend Ilana deserves all the credit for naming this dish. Gehakte leber in Yiddish is chopped liver. Memories of my childhood and early teens come racing to mind when making or just thinking about chopped liver. It's prepared by gently sautéing chicken livers and onions in chicken schmaltz, and then combining with chopped boiled eggs, and blending finely to make a rich, smooth pate. Sacrilege to this traditional recipe, you'll see bacon here, but it works so well with this dish that I couldn't resist.

Ingredients – makes approximately 4 cups

2 teaspoons schmaltz (rendered chicken fat) or light olive oil

1 large brown onion, finely chopped

400g chicken livers, each piece cut in half, sinew removed and discarded

Pinch dried thyme leaves, or a few fresh picked leaves

Sea salt and freshly ground black pepper

2 tablespoons parsley, finely chopped

8 large toasted walnuts and extra toasted crushed walnuts, for garnish

¼ teaspoon lemon zest (optional)

5 large hard-boiled **eggs**

4 rindless streaky **bacon** rashers, sliced very thin

 **CHOOK'S TIPS**

Before serving, don't forget to remove the toothpicks. Rendered chicken fat is used in making traditional chopped liver. You can render your own chicken schmaltz when you make your own chicken stock. The flavour it brings to this dish is quite unique and well worth trying. Chopped liver pate will store well in the fridge in an airtight container for 3 days.

Method

In a medium frying pan, heat the chicken schmaltz or oil over low heat and cook the onions for 25 - 30 minutes, stirring frequently. Remove onions and set aside. Turn the heat up to medium, and in the same frying pan, add the chicken livers, thyme, salt and pepper and cook for 3 minutes on each side, or until cooked through, but not overdone. Place the liver, cooked onions and walnuts in a food processor and blend with 4 of the hard-boiled eggs. Place into a bowl and stir through the parsley and lemon zest, if using. Check the seasoning at this point and adjust if required. Wipe the frying pan clean and cook the bacon over medium heat on both sides until just browned, but still moist and pliable. Drain on paper towels until cool enough to handle. Place a molded mound of chopped liver onto a serving plate. Wrap a piece of bacon around the girth of the mound and secure with a toothpick. Finely grate the remaining boiled egg and sprinkle on top of the chopped liver, with extra walnuts and a pinch of fresh thyme leaves or extra parsley.

Brunch & Anytime Snacks

Peking Porky

Chinese is one of my favourite cuisines, and especially a great Peking duck is certainly on order every time. Crispy skin, succulent flesh, thin egg pancakes, crunchy cucumber and that delicious sauce that brings it all together – so good! Try this fabulous version using store bought barbecue pork. It's so simple to make. Double the quantities, because they'll go fast!

Ingredients – serves 4 as entrée

1 packet Peking duck **pancake** wrappers, containing 12 pancakes

1 large Lebanese cucumber, seeds removed, sliced and cut into 5cm lengths

400g char siu barbecue **pork**, sliced to 1cm thickness, and cut into 5cm lengths

4 thin spring onions, cut into 5cm lengths

1 tablespoon hoisin sauce, or more, depending on taste

Method

Prepare the duck wrappers as per packet instructions. Lay the wrappers on a clean surface. On each wrapper, smear 1 teaspoon hoisin sauce along the centre of each pancake. Following the line of the sauce, place some cucumber, spring onions and barbecue pork on top of the hoisin. Starting at one end, gently roll the wrapper to enclose the parcel. Serve immediately.

CHOOK'S TIPS

To enhance the flavours of this dish, make sure you warm the char siu barbecue pork before preparation. Room temperature is fine too, as long as the meat isn't served straight from the fridge, otherwise flavours are not as pronounced. For a milder onion taste, substitute the spring onions with garlic chives.

Peking Chook: As an option, you can use barbecue or poached chicken.

Peking Snapper or Ling: I have also made these pancakes with Asian style poached snapper, picking selected chunks of juicy flesh to accompany the cucumber and hoisin, and added a little coriander for extra freshness.

Brunch & Anytime Snacks

Asparagus, Prosciutto & Eggs Mimosa

This is one of the simplest meals to prepare. It's quick, super delicious and is an impressive entrée at a dinner party. Just increase quantities to suit number of guests.

Ingredients – makes 4 servings

1 bunch fresh asparagus, ends trimmed, 8 asparagus spears required

8 slices of **prosciutto**, room temperature

4 hard-boiled **eggs**, peeled, egg yolks and egg whites separated

Extra virgin olive oil, to drizzle

Method

Using a fine grater or zester, grate the egg whites into a bowl. Grate the yolks into a separate bowl and set aside. Bring a medium saucepan of water to the boil. Add asparagus spears and blanch for about 3 - 4 minutes, depending on thickness. Place the asparagus into a bowl of ice water for 1 minute. This will stop the cooking process and retain the vibrant colour of the asparagus. Drain well on paper towels and arrange the prosciutto and asparagus on plates. Sprinkle the egg whites over the asparagus and prosciutto, then top with the egg yolks. Drizzle with some olive oil and serve.

 **CHOOK'S TIPS**

A great vegetarian alternative to this dish is to use lightly pan-fried eggplant slices in lieu of the prosciutto.

35

Brunch & Anytime Snacks

Eggs Kilpatrick

Oysters Kilpatrick is a very popular dish, made with a bacon and Worcestershire sauce dressing, liberally drizzled over freshly shucked oysters. A dozen oysters are never enough, I can always eat more. Here's my clever, less expensive version using the famous dressing on eggs – 'Googy Eggs Kilpatrick'. The following recipes will surprise you with their simplistic preparation and great taste.

Ingredients – makes 24 single serves

12 large hard-boiled **eggs**, peeled and halved lengthways.
6 rindless **bacon** rashers, finely cut into match sticks
2 tablespoons Worcestershire sauce
Lemon wedges and rocket, for serving

Method

In a medium frying pan, cook the bacon until browned all over. Drain well. Mix bacon and Worcestershire sauce in a bowl. Arrange the eggs on a serving plate cut side up. Carefully place a heaped teaspoon of bacon mixture on top of the eggs and serve with rocket and lemon wedges. For a richer, sweeter flavour, you can add a tablespoon of barbecue sauce to the Worcestershire sauce and gently warm the two ingredients and the bacon in a small saucepan before pouring over the eggs.

Devilled Eggs Kilpatrick

Ingredients – makes 24 single serves

12 large hard-boiled **eggs**, peeled and halved lengthways
6 rindless **bacon** rashers, finely cut into match sticks, reserving a little for garnish
2 tablespoons Worcestershire sauce
1 teaspoon English mustard
2 tablespoons whole-**egg** mayonnaise

 **CHOOK'S TIPS**

Devilled eggs travel well when packed neatly into a sealed container. Place them on some shredded lettuce or rocket to stop them sliding around in the container. They also keep well in a sealed container in the fridge, so they can be made in advance.

Method

In a medium frying pan, cook the bacon until browned all over. Drain well. Separate the egg yolks from the egg whites. Gently rinse the egg whites and pat dry. Place the rocket on a serving plate. Arrange the egg white shells on top. Mix the mayonnaise, mustard, crumbled egg yolks and Worcestershire sauce in a bowl until you have a smooth, lump free consistency. Gently fold in the bacon. Place a heaped teaspoon or more of kilpatrick mixture into the egg white shells. Garnish with remaining bacon matchsticks and a few drops of Worcestershire sauce and serve.

Brunch & Anytime Snacks

Scotch Eggs

When I think of scotch eggs, I think picnics, lunch boxes, party food and snacks on the run.....these are a great all round filler and very moreish. Easy to make and they last in the fridge for days covered in an airtight container. Like meatloaf or a bolognese sauce, this is an excellent way to sneak a few vegetables into the mix and the kids won't even know.

Ingredients – makes 8

500g quality **sausage** meat
1 medium carrot, finely minced
1 stick celery, finely minced
1 small brown onion, peeled and finely minced
Few sprigs parsley, finely chopped
Sea salt and black pepper for seasoning
Pinch dried sage (optional)
8 large medium-boiled **eggs**, peeled, rinsed and wiped dry
Plain flour, for coating
2 large **eggs**, beaten
Fine breadcrumbs for coating
Vegetable oil for deep frying

Method

In a large bowl, thoroughly mix the sausage meat, minced vegetables, parsley, seasoning, and sage, if using. Divide mixture into 8 equal portions. Roll out each portion to approximately 1cm thickness into ovals and carefully wrap around each egg, sealing edges well. Repeat with the other remaining eggs and sausage mixture. Place the plain flour, eggs and breadcrumbs in 3 separate bowls. Using one 'wet' hand, dredge each prepared egg in the flour to completely cover it, then into the beaten eggs and then place into the crumbs. With the 'dry' hand, coat the eggs well in the breadcrumbs. Set aside. Preheat the oven to 180°C. Heat the oil in a medium saucepan over medium - high heat. When oil is hot enough to turn a cube of bread brown in approximately 30 seconds, cook 2 eggs at a time, for approximately 4 – 5 minutes using a wooden spoon to gently turn the eggs in the oil so they cook evenly. Remove with slotted spoon, drain on paper towels and place on a baking tray. Cover loosely with foil and bake for a further 8 - 10 minutes to ensure the meat is completely cooked through. Test one after 8 minutes by cutting in half. The Scotch Eggs are perfectly cooked if the meat has no pink tinge and juices run clear. If they're not cooked, return to the oven and bake for a further few minutes, until completely cooked through. Vegetarians, try using falafel mixture instead of the sausage meat. This is such a tasty alternative.

Brunch & Anytime Snacks

Ham & Mushroom Crepes

Perfect for a buffet brunch or even a light main, these sumptuous crepes are really tasty. The filling is made with a white sauce (Béchamel) base, and there's no limit to the ingredients you can use to fill your crepes.

Ingredients – makes 8 crepes

1½ cups prepared white sauce
2 cups sliced **ham**, shredded
2 tablespoons prepared onion confit (cooked, caramelised onion)
2 cups cooked, sliced button mushrooms
Sea salt and freshly ground black pepper
Chopped parsley, for garnish
8 medium **crepes** – recipe to follow

Crepes – makes 8-10

1 cup plain flour, sifted
3 large **eggs**
2 cups milk
50g melted butter, cooled, plus extra for greasing
½ teaspoon salt

 **CHOOK'S TIPS**

Vegetarians can substitute the ham for a trio of mushrooms such as Swiss brown, button and portobello, or char-grilled zucchini and artichokes hearts also work well. Chicken and prawns are also great alternatives to the ham. Add a little hot English mustard to the white sauce to spice things up a bit.

Method

Crepes:

Sift the flour and the salt into a bowl. Combine the eggs, milk and butter in a jug and slowly whisk into the flour until you have a smooth, lump free consistency. Allow batter to rest for 20 minutes. Heat a medium size crepe pan over medium heat. Lightly grease the pan with some of the butter. Pour in just enough crepe mixture (about 1/3 cup) to evenly coat the pan with a thin layer of batter. Cook on one side for approximately 30 - 40 seconds or until little air bubbles start to form on the top and base of crepe is browned, then flip and cook the other side for a further 20 seconds or until lightly browned and cooked through. Set aside on a large plate. Repeat with remaining batter.

Sauce:

Warm the white sauce in a small saucepan. You may need to add a few drops of water or chicken stock to loosen it if it's too thick. The sauce should be a 'dollopy' consistency like a good mayonnaise – not too thick and not too runny. Stir in the ham, onion confit and mushrooms and mix well.

Pre-heat the oven to 180°C. Place 1 crepe on a clean surface and spoon approximately ½ a cup mixture along the centre. Roll crepe gently but firmly. Place seam side down in an oven proof dish. Repeat with remaining crepes and mixture. Cover lightly with foil and warm the crepes for 15 - 18 minutes. Garnish with a sprinkle of parsley and serve immediately with salad. If there's any leftover ham and mushroom sauce, you can pour it over the crepes before serving.

Brunch & Anytime Snacks

Ricotta & Bacon Hotcakes

Speaking from personal experience, these hotcakes are so good that you'll probably want to double the quantity, because you'll eat half of them before anyone else gets a chance.

Ingredients – makes 20-24

400g ricotta cheese
3 large fresh **eggs**
Sea salt and freshly ground black pepper
2 fresh sage leaves, finely sliced
3 tablespoons self-raising flour, sifted
Pinch of baking soda
1 cup **bacon**, cooked and finely chopped
Vegetable oil for shallow frying

Method

Combine the ricotta, eggs, salt, pepper, sage, flour and baking soda together. Stir in the bacon. Heat a little oil in a frying pan over medium-high heat. Drop tablespoons of batter into the frying pan, allowing room for spreading. Cook for approximately 2 minutes on each side, or until golden and brown and cooked through. Drain on paper towels. Repeat with the remaining mixture. Serve hot or at room temperature.

CHOOK'S TIPS

I've also made this recipe using the batter as a filling in filo pastry cases, using a 12 hole medium size muffin tray. Ricotta hotcakes can be refrigerated in an airtight container for up to 3 days. To reheat, place in a microwave proof container, or wrap in foil and warm in the oven. For a vegetarian, sweet version of the hotcakes, leave out the bacon and baking soda and add 1 teaspoon nutmeg and 3 tablespoons caster sugar to the mixture. Follow the cooking steps as shown above.

Brunch & Anytime Snacks

Little Pork Balls with Coriander & Lime Dipping Sauce

My live-in students influence many of the meals I prepare in the house, and as pork is one of their favourite meats, they are constantly asking me to make these little pork balls. They pack well in school lunch boxes and they're deliciously moreish. The spicy sauce is a perfect partner.

Ingredients – makes 20-24 servings

500g lean **pork mince**

½ cup Asian shallots, minced

1 large fresh **egg**

¼ cup coriander leaves and roots, finely chopped

¼ cup breadcrumbs

75g tinned water chestnuts, rinsed, drained and finely chopped

Sea salt and freshly ground black pepper

Peanut oil for shallow frying

Coriander & Lime Dipping Sauce

1 teaspoon fish sauce 1 tablespoon dark brown sugar

1 tablespoon fresh lime juice

¼ teaspoon freshly grated lime zest

1 red chilli, seeded and finely chopped

¼ cup coriander leaves, finely chopped, plus extra picked leaves, for garnish

Method

Dipping Sauce:

Combine all the ingredients and set aside.

Pork Balls:

Combine all the ingredients except the peanut oil, and mix thoroughly. Refrigerate for 20 minutes to firm. This makes handling easier. With wet hands, roll mince into golf ball size pieces. Heat the oil in a large frying pan over medium - high heat and cook in 2 batches, turning frequently, until well browned and cooked through, about 10 minutes. The pork balls are cooked when the juices run clear. Place onto serving plate with dipping sauce on the side.

 **CHOOK'S TIPS**

These work really well with fish, prawn or chicken mince. Use exactly the same quantities of protein and apply the same method in preparation.

Brunch & Anytime Snacks

Omelette Sang Choy Bow

A favourite entrée for many when dining out Chinese style is Sang Choy Bow and it's certainly one of my favourites. Wrapping the cold lettuce and hot meat mix in an Asian flavoured omelette is an innovative variation on this recipe with a zillion versions.

Ingredients - makes 4 parcels

6 large **eggs**

1 tablespoon dark soy

1½ teaspoons sesame oil

2 tablespoons peanut oil, or more if required

400g lean **pork mince**

½ small red chilli, seeded and finely chopped

2 cloves garlic, minced

1 teaspoon fresh ginger, minced

1 Asian shallot, finely chopped

1 tablespoon oyster sauce

1 tablespoon hoisin sauce

1 tablespoon light soy

100g tinned water chestnuts, rinsed, drained and finely chopped

1 cup carrot, coarsely grated

6 large, dried shiitake mushrooms, rehydrated in boiling water and thinly sliced, woody stems discarded

1 cup celery, finely chopped

½ cup strong flavoured chicken stock, or more as required

1 tablespoon corn flour mixed with 1 tablespoon water to make a paste

1 cup fresh bean shoots, ragged ends trimmed

4 spring onions, green part only, finely sliced on the diagonal

¼ cup finely shredded iceberg or cos lettuce per serve

8 garlic chives blanched in boiling water for 1 minute, drained and set aside

Method

Omelettes:

Combine the eggs with the dark soy and ½ teaspoon of the sesame oil. Heat 1 teaspoon of peanut oil in a large crepe pan over medium - high heat. Place ¼ of the egg mixture into the pan, swirling to coat the base of the pan. Cook until just set. Set aside and repeat to make 4 omelette crepes.

Filling:

Heat remaining peanut oil in a wok over medium - high heat and brown the mince. Add remaining sesame oil, chilli, garlic, ginger and shallots and cook for a further 2 minutes. Add oyster, hoisin and light soy sauces, and cook for another minute. Add the water chestnuts, carrot, mushrooms, celery, stock and corn flour paste. Turn heat to low, and allow the flavours to infuse, approximately 3 - 4 minutes, stirring gently. Taste for seasoning. Adjust if necessary with extra light soy or stock. Drain excess liquid and reserve as stock for later use.

Lay 1 omelette on a plate and place ¼ cup lettuce in the middle of the crepe and ¼ cup filling on top. Carefully bring the edges of the crepe together to make a 'money bag' parcel and tie securely with a blanched garlic chive. Don't pull the chives too tight or they may break and be careful not to overfill. Alternatively you can fold the omelette edges over each other to make a parcel, as you would make a spring roll. Serve immediately.

CHOOK'S TIPS

Alternative proteins to pork mince that I've tried with this recipe are chicken and prawn, which are equally as good. A great vegetarian alternative would be to leave out the pork mince and use extra grated carrot, water chestnuts and thinly sliced bamboo shoots. The filling, without bean sprouts or lettuce, can be frozen in airtight containers for up to a month.

Salads

Salads

Pink Salad with Mascarpone & Cumin Dressing

This is a beautiful summer salad that's not only pretty – it's delicious and very healthy. You'll need to start this recipe the day before if using fresh beetroot. The beetroot and watermelon combo is superb and together with a 'top shelf' prosciutto, this will be the show-stopper on any table.

Ingredients - serves 8

400g beetroot, chopped into bite size pieces, or a 400g jar of store bought baby beetroot
8 hard-boiled **eggs**, peeled and rinsed
16 slices **prosciutto**
½ small red cabbage, finely shredded
1 tablespoon extra virgin olive oil
½ Spanish onion, finely sliced
3 radishes, finely sliced
1 red dragon fruit, chopped into bite size pieces
300g watermelon, chopped into bite size pieces
200g red cherries

Mascarpone & Cumin Dressing:

125g mascarpone cheese, room temperature
1-1½ teaspoons ground cumin
2 tablespoons light olive oil
Sea salt and freshly ground black pepper

CHOOK'S TIPS

You don't have to limit this salad to the summer months. Choose seasonal fruits and design your own Pink Salad. It's also delicious with char-grilled eggplant and a good Greek, Danish or Australian feta. Store bought jars of baby beetroot provide gorgeous little bite size baby beetroot pieces and a really vibrant pink liquid for the boiled eggs, so if you want the pinkest eggs ever…..

Method

If using fresh beetroot, the day before serving, place unpeeled beetroots in a small pot of water and bring to the boil. Lower heat and simmer for 25 minutes or until cooked through. Remove the beetroots, and refrigerate the 'pink' water in a sealed container. When the beetroots are cool enough to handle, peel and discard skins. (You can skip this step if using store bought beetroot).

Submerge the hard-boiled eggs into a container with enough of the pink water so the eggs are completely covered. Seal and refrigerate for 24 hours.

For the dressing:

Combine the mascarpone cheese with the olive oil, cumin, salt and pepper. Season and set aside covered at room temperature. The mixture should be a 'dollopy' consistency like a good mayonnaise – not too thick and not too runny. Bring the prosciutto to room temperature. Bring a medium saucepan of water to the boil. Wilt the cabbage for 1 minute, drain well and set aside. Line the serving plate with the cabbage. Drizzle with some extra virgin olive oil, a little salt and pepper and toss to combine. Scatter the beetroot, onion rings, radish slices, prosciutto, and fruits of choice over the cabbage. Remove the eggs from the pink water and wipe dry. Cut eggs in half width ways and nestle them on top of the salad. Randomly dollop the mascarpone dressing over the salad and serve.

Salads

Caesar Salad Fresh Spring Rolls

Fresh, light and healthy, this is such a unique way to serve a Caesar salad. Rice paper wrappers are really versatile – try using them for other salads such as BLT, waldorf and the Indonesian favourite, gado gado. I've even used them for left over risotto and added some croutons and lettuce for crunch.

Ingredients
– makes 20 - 22 rolls approximately

1 cup whole **egg** mayonnaise

2 cloves garlic, minced

6 anchovies, finely chopped

6 slices pane di casa bread, crusts discarded, bread cut into 1cm croutons

2 tablespoons light olive oil

2 cooked chicken breasts, shredded

8 rindless short-cut **bacon** rashers, chopped into lardons, fried until crispy, drained well

4 large hard-boiled **eggs**, peeled, rinsed and chopped

1 packet of medium sized rice paper spring roll wrappers

1 medium cos lettuce, washed, dried and finely shredded

 **CHOOK'S TIPS**

These delicious parcels should be served straight away, as the croutons won't stay crunchy for too long once they come in contact with the 'wet' filling. A lemon and anchovy vinaigrette also works well as a dipping sauce.

Method

Anchovy Mayonnaise:

Combine the mayonnaise, garlic and anchovies.

Filling:

Heat the olive oil in medium frying pan and toast the croutons, tossing regularly until browned and crispy. Set aside. Prepare work surface. Dampen a clean absorbent cloth or tea towel, and place onto a clean work surface. In a large bowl, combine the chicken, bacon, chopped egg and about half of the anchovy mayonnaise, or more if required.

Fill another large bowl with warm water. Working quickly, take 1 rice paper wrapper at a time, and completely submerge in the water for 3 seconds. Place it on the cloth and allow it to soften, about 30 seconds. Repeat with another 2 wrappers, laying them next to each other. By this time, the first wrapper should be pliable enough to work with. Using tongs, place a small amount of lettuce in the middle of the wrapper. Add approximately 1½ tablespoons of the filling and top with a few croutons. Roll the fresh spring roll carefully, folding in the sides as you go. Set aside onto the serving plate. Repeat with remaining ingredients, leaving a small space in between each spring roll, as they tend to stick together. Serve immediately with remaining anchovy mayonnaise.

Salads

BLT in a Bowl

The humble BLT is a very popular bacon, lettuce and tomato sandwich, found in most western countries around the world in street cafes and 5 star hotels alike. Lustful bacon cravings will be fulfilled with this fresh and innovative BLT salad in a Bowl.

Ingredients - serves 8

8 rindless short-cut **bacon** rashers, chopped into lardons, fried until crispy, drained well

6 slices pane di casa bread, crusts discarded, bread cut into 1cm croutons

1 - 2 tablespoons light olive oil

¾ cup mustard **mayonnaise** - recipe to follow

2 punnets large cherry tomatoes, washed, dried and halved

1 small iceberg or bibb lettuce, washed and roughly torn, dark outer leaves discarded

Mustard Mayonnaise:

Combine 1 cup whole-**egg** mayonnaise and 1½ tablespoons Dijon or grainy mustard. Cover and set aside in the fridge until required.

Method

Filling:

Heat the olive oil in medium frying pan and toast the croutons, tossing regularly until browned and crispy. Set aside. In a medium bowl, combine 2 tablespoons of the prepared mustard mayonnaise with the tomatoes and mix until evenly coated. Place the lettuce into individual bowls, and add the tomatoes. Scatter the bacon and croutons over the top. Drizzle with a little more mustard mayonnaise and serve immediately. To make a main meal, add some boiled eggs and avocado for a B.L.E.A.T.

CHOOK'S TIPS

Turkey and chicken breast are wonderful alternatives to bacon in this salad. As a delicious vegetarian version, omit the bacon and add slices of char-grilled eggplant and thin slices of Spanish onion for an E.O.L.T, and my favourite, a P.L.A.T, using cooked king prawns and avocado with a seafood cocktail sauce in lieu of the mustard mayonnaise.

Salads

Potato Salad with Bacon & Egg

Who doesn't like potato salad! I think everyone has an affinity for this classic. Great for a barbecue with the chops, or partnered with a Sunday roast and it's the perfect complement to garden salads. There are many variations of this staple, and this one is simple to make and packed full of flavour.

Ingredients – makes 8 servings

1½ kg all-purpose potatoes, peeled and chopped into bite size pieces

10 rindless short-cut **bacon** rashers, roughly chopped, fried until crispy, drained well

1 cup whole-**egg** mayonnaise or more if required

8 spring onions, sliced finely on the diagonal, reserving a few for garnish

Sea salt and freshly ground black pepper

10 hard-boiled **eggs**, peeled, rinsed and quartered

Method

Place the potatoes in a large pot and cover with water. Add 1 tablespoon of cooking salt and bring to the boil. Cook until the potatoes are just cooked through. Drain well and place potatoes back in the cooking pot, allowing any excess water to dissipate. In a large bowl, combine the potatoes, bacon, mayonnaise, spring onions, a pinch of sea salt and pepper. Add the egg quarters and give another gentle stir. Garnish with the remaining spring onions.

 CHOOK'S TIPS

Don't overcook the potatoes or you'll end up with mash. In the event of this happening, (and I know this because it's happened to me more than once), omit the mayo and add some thickened cream or hot milk and some butter to make perfect mash. Place the eggs on top, scatter the bacon over and garnish with the spring onions. Don't forget the water has been salted and the bacon is salty, so keep this in mind when seasoning.

Note: My mum makes a terrific Asian potato salad. Add a few drops of sesame oil to the mayonnaise, and mix thoroughly before stirring it through the potatoes. Add the eggs, and sprinkle with toasted sesame seeds and spring onions. I've taken mum's Asian potato salad one step further, with the addition of chopped, store-bought char siu barbecue pork – mighty fine tucker! Potato salad without the spring onion stores really well in the fridge for up to 3 days in a sealed container, so it's perfect to make in advance.

Salads

Succotash Salad

Succotash and I are best friends; I just love it. It's a popular salad in the United States, as ever-present on the dinner table as a potato salad is at an Aussie barbecue. Usually served as a side salad, the juicy sweet corn, salty bacon bits, creamy broad beans and green capsicum (for super crunch), melt taste buds when combined in this appetising salad.

Ingredients – makes 8 small servings or 4 large

500g packet frozen broad beans

2 fresh ears of corn, cooked, or 2 cups tinned corn, drained

6 rindless short-cut **bacon** rashers, roughly chopped, fried until crispy, drained well

1 cup green capsicum, diced

½ cup chopped parsley or coriander

½ Spanish onion, finely chopped

4 large hard-boiled **eggs**

Dressing

1 tablespoon Dijon mustard

2 - 3 tablespoons lemon juice

2 tablespoons extra virgin olive oil

Sea salt and freshly ground black pepper

Method

Dressing:

Combine all the ingredients and set aside until required.

Salad:

Cook the broad beans according to packet instructions. Allow to cool, shell the beans, discarding outer skins.

In a mixing bowl, combine the broad beans, corn, bacon and capsicum, parsley or coriander and onion. Season as required, add the salad dressing and toss to combine. Serve with hard-boiled eggs.

CHOOK'S TIPS

Many succotash recipes I've tried include cream and quite a lot of it too. I haven't included cream in this recipe, as I think it's too heavy and takes away from the simple freshness of this salad, so opt for the vinaigrette based dressing instead.

Another great variation is to substitute the bacon for some spicy **chorizo**, sliced thinly and pan-fried until the fragrant oils start to release. For a vegetarian style succotash, you can substitute the bacon for roasted sweet potato. This dish is a great accompaniment to any poultry, fish, steak or baked dinner.

Salads

Israeli Salad & Boiled Eggs

Memories of my grandmother making this vibrant salad make me smile. Oma's eggs were always overcooked, more like way overdone really, but the meal itself was delicious. The little jewels of peppery radish crunch complement the eggs perfectly, no matter how they are cooked.

Ingredients – serves 4

4 medium radishes, finely diced
1 telegraph cucumber, seeded and finely diced
3 firm Roma tomatoes, seeded and finely diced
3 spring onions, finely sliced
1/3 cup flat leaf parsley, finely chopped
8 large fresh **eggs**, boiled for 4 minutes, immersed in cold water, and peeled
400g **salami** or **wurst** pan-fried, for serving

Dressing

2 tablespoons extra virgin olive oil
1 large lemon, juiced, seeds discarded
Sea salt and freshly ground black pepper

Method

Dressing:

Combine all the ingredients well and set aside until required.

Salad:

In a medium bowl, combine the radishes, cucumber, tomatoes, spring onions and parsley. Add the dressing and gently combine. Divide salad onto small serving plates or into small bowls. Halve the eggs and place on top of the salad. Serve immediately with the pan-fried salami or wurst.

CHOOK'S TIPS

For this recipe, I like to leave the skin on the vegetables. As well as being highly nutritious, it provides added colour and vibrancy to the salad. An alternative serving suggestion is to fill some warmed fresh pita bread pockets with the salad and eggs. Add a little cooked, diced chicken or even some chopped falafel balls and you've got a brilliant meal. You can prepare the salad a few hours ahead of time, as this salad won't go super soggy. Cover and refrigerate until required. Dress salad just before serving.

Recently I had lunch at my friends, Ilana and David's house. Ilana made a cracking good Israeli salad, so good in fact that it has to get a mention. Ilana adds grated carrot, finely chopped Spanish onion and a mix of red, green and yellow capsicums. Honestly one of the best I've ever had. In Ilana's words…"it's all in the tiny chopping".

Noodles / Pasta / Rice

Noodles / Pasta / Rice

Californian Rolls with BBQ Pork & Egg Salad

These special rolls are so tasty, easy to prepare and they don't take long to make – just a few basic steps to follow. My international students love these so I find myself making them at least once a week for their lunches.

Ingredients – makes 4 full rolls or 16 pieces approximately

1½ cups Japanese sushi rice or other short grain rice

1 tablespoon rice wine vinegar

4 sheets nori paper

200g char siu barbecue **pork**, finely chopped

2 large **eggs**, cooked as an omelette, cut into strips, or ½ cup **egg** salad - recipe to follow

1 Lebanese cucumber, cut into 3cm lengths

Japanese seaweed salad, for serving

Japanese rice seasoning, for garnish (optional)

Wasabi paste, for serving

Japanese soy sauce, for serving

Method

Cook rice as per packet instructions and cool. Combine the rice and wine vinegar and mix thoroughly. Lay one nori sheet flat onto a sushi rolling mat, shiny side down, making sure the lines of the sheet are longitudinal. Place a layer of rice over ¾ of the sheet starting at the end closest to you, leaving a 1cm border.

In the centre of the rice, horizontally lay some barbecue pork and omelette strips, or small spoonfuls of egg salad if using, along the rice. Gently lift the rolling mat at the edge closest to you and roll tightly. Wet the nori paper along the far edge and seal together. Cut into pieces along the marked lines of the nori paper. Discard the ragged ends (I usually eat them) and arrange the rolls on a plate. Top half the rolls with Japanese seaweed salad. Sprinkle a little rice seasoning, if using, on each roll and serve with wasabi and soy.

Egg Salad

Hard boil 4 large **eggs**, peel and rinse thoroughly, then finely chop them into a bowl. (I blend them in a food processor with a few short bursts, which gives a smoother consistency). Add 1 tablespoon of whole-**egg** mayonnaise and season with sea salt flakes and white pepper.

Flavour Options: Sometimes I add a teaspoon of onion confit (cooked, caramelised onions) to the egg salad to enhance flavour. A few chopped chives can also be substituted for the onion confit.

CHOOK'S TIPS

Barbecue pork can be substituted with cooked chicken or beef, marinated in a teriyaki sauce. Rolling mats and Japanese rice seasoning are available from Asian grocery stores.

Noodles / Pasta / Rice

Singapore Noodles with Pork & Egg Threads

This is one of my all-time favourite noodle dishes — ever, and definitely one I could probably eat every day. One of the restaurants in Melbourne's Chinatown makes an excellent version, so one day I asked a waiter if there was any chance I could watch the chef make this? Lucky me, he said "yes".

Ingredients - serves 4

250g packet rice vermicelli

3 large **eggs**, lightly beaten

2 - 3 tablespoons peanut oil

1 large brown onion, peeled and sliced into thin wedges

2 cloves garlic, minced

1 tablespoon fresh ginger, minced

1 teaspoon sesame oil, or more depending on taste

2 tablespoon curry powder

1 teaspoon turmeric powder

1 green capsicum, seeded and sliced

400g char siu barbecue **pork**, diced into 1cm pieces

½ cup strong flavoured chicken stock

1 - 2 tablespoons Japanese soy sauce

1 cup snow peas, ends trimmed and cut in thirds on the diagonal

1 large carrot, grated, or chopped into matchsticks

1 cup bean sprouts (optional)

 CHOOK'S TIPS

Vermicelli noodles are temperamental, so it's important not to overcook them in the initial stages. This dish sometimes includes minced pork, red capsicum, and prawns. I prefer the green capsicum with this dish, but you can try all of the above. If you like your food spicy, add more curry powder and turmeric to taste. If you have any left overs, these noodles are great wrapped in rice paper rolls and served as a snack.

Method

Place the vermicelli rice noodles in a large bowl and cover with boiling water. Leave for 2 minutes or until just starting to soften. Rinse in cold water. Set aside to cool and drain completely. In a large, deep non-stick frying pan or wok, heat 1 teaspoon of oil over medium - high heat and cook the eggs until firm. Cut into thin strips and set aside. In the same frying pan or wok, heat 1 tablespoon of the oil over medium - high heat and cook the onion, garlic, ginger, sesame oil, curry and turmeric powders until fragrant, about 1 minute. Add capsicum, pork, chicken stock and soy. Continue cooking for approximately 2 minutes, then add the omelette strips, carrot, snow peas and bean sprouts, if using. Gently toss for another minute so all ingredients are coated with sauce. Turn the heat off and set the frying pan or wok aside.

Place noodles into the large bowl. Combine the cooked ingredients and mix thoroughly. Alternatively, you can place all the ingredients back into the wok and heat, tossing gently to combine, ensuring all the noodles are coated with sauce. You may need to add a little extra stock or soy (or both) if the noodles are too dry.

Noodles / Pasta / Rice

Pearl Couscous Carbonara

Spaghetti Carbonara, the pasta dish with a thousand versions — it's one of those meals that make your mouth water just thinking about it, and if you master this recipe, it gets you lots of brownie points with friends and family. Here's my version, made with mascarpone cream cheese, loads of garlic and I've replaced the traditional spaghetti pasta with pearl couscous.

Ingredients - serves 4

1 tablespoon olive oil

8 rindless bacon **rashers**, diced or equal quantity of diced speck, approximately 400g

1 medium brown onion, finely chopped

4 cloves garlic, minced

1 packet pearl (Israeli) couscous

100g mascarpone or cream cheese, softened to room temperature

100ml thickened cream

2 large **eggs** and 1 **egg yolk**

1 teaspoon freshly ground black pepper

1/3 cup parmesan cheese, freshly grated plus extra for sprinkling

1 tablespoon parsley, finely chopped

Method

Heat the oil in a large frying pan over medium - high heat. Add bacon or speck and onion, and cook until the bacon is browned and the onions are translucent, about 4 - 5 minutes. Add the garlic and cook for a further minute until fragrant. Remove pan from heat and set aside. Meanwhile, bring a large saucepan of salted water to the boil and cook the couscous until al dente. Drain well and set aside. Don't rinse the couscous.

In a separate bowl, combine mascarpone or cream cheese, cream, eggs and yolk, pepper and parmesan cheese. Place the frying pan over medium heat. Place the couscous and the bacon mixture in the pan and add the cream cheese and egg mixture. Gently toss for 1 - 2 minutes or until eggs start to thicken the sauce and evenly coat the couscous. Ladle into bowls and garnish with additional parmesan and parsley.

 **CHOOK'S TIPS**

You can loosen the sauce with a little water or chicken stock if the sauce becomes too thick. Be sure the pan is not too hot when you add the egg mixture otherwise it may set like an omelette.

If you want creamier pasta, just add as much cream as desired to the egg and cheese mixture. This dish can be easily substituted to suit vegetarian palates by replacing the bacon with cooked zucchini pieces, broccoli, mushrooms or any other of your favourite vegetables. I have also made this dish substituting the bacon for prawns - very, very good!

Noodles / Pasta / Rice

Risotto with Pancetta, Bacon & Poached Eggs

Creating a risotto is like having a blank canvas and a supply of fresh produce for paint. This risotto is the perfect winter lunch or dinner – it's full of flavour and really hearty. If you are a risotto fan, you will love this Pancetta, Bacon & Egg version.

Ingredients - serves 2

2 teaspoons olive oil
2 teaspoons butter (optional)
200g **pancetta** slices
200g rindless short-cut **bacon**, chopped into lardons
1 brown onion, finely chopped or 1 medium leek, finely sliced, white and light green parts only
1 cup arborio or other short grain, starchy rice
1/3 cup dry white wine
4 cups strong flavoured chicken stock, warmed, plus a little extra stock or water if required
Sea salt and freshly ground black pepper
2 large poached **eggs**, for serving
1 tablespoon parsley, finely chopped
Parmesan cheese, grated (optional)

Method

Heat 1 teaspoon of the oil in a large saucepan over medium - high heat and cook the pancetta until browned and crispy, approximately 1 minute. Drain on paper towels and set aside. In the same saucepan, cook the bacon until browned and crispy. Drain and set aside separate to the pancetta. Add the remaining oil, and butter if using, and cook the onion or leek over medium - high heat until soft, fragrant and translucent, stirring constantly, about 4 minutes. Add the rice and stir to completely coat all the rice grains. When the rice is crackling hot, add the wine and ½ cup stock together and stir once only. When most of the liquid has evaporated, add remaining stock, 1 cup at a time, allowing the moisture to absorb between additions. Stir gently thereafter each addition of stock. Continue cooking until rice is cooked through, a further 15 - 20 minutes. Taste and season as required. Towards the end of cooking time, stir the reserved bacon through the risotto. Use the additional stock or water if risotto requires more liquid. Serve immediately in bowls, topped with reserved pancetta, poached eggs, a sprinkle of parsley and parmesan, if using.

 **CHOOK'S TIPS**

The possibilities with risotto are infinite, as are vegetarian options. Some delicious suggestions are beetroot and goats cheese, mushrooms and tomatoes, leek, cauliflower and cheese, pumpkin and sage with toasted almond slivers, and using vegetable stock in lieu of the chicken stock. Whatever your favourite ingredients are, try them in a risotto; just stick to the basic measurements of rice to stock quantities as shown here.

Noodles / Pasta / Rice

Kedgeree

Kedgeree is a wonderful dish, a staple relic of Britain's Indian Colonial past. Originally served for breakfast, it also makes a fantastic lunch or main meal. Traditionally smoked cod or haddock is poached in milk and fragrant spices and stirred through cooked rice, with boiled eggs added at the end. I've created a much simpler version using smoked trout, as it works particularly well in Kedgeree.

Ingredients – serves 4

2 cups fish stock, or 2 fish stock cubes and 2 cups water
2 additional cups water
2 teaspoons curry powder
1/3 cup onion confit (cooked, caramelised onion)
1 dried bay leaf
1 dried curry leaf
1½ cups basmati rice
4 medium-boiled **eggs**, quartered
400g smoked trout
2 tablespoons flat leaf parsley, finely chopped
Freshly ground black pepper, to serve
Lemon wedges, to serve

Method

In a large deep saucepan, bring the stock and water to the boil. Add the curry powder, onion confit, and bay and curry leaves. Season with a pinch of sea salt and add the rice. Turn heat down to low and let the rice simmer for approximately 15 minutes, stirring occasionally, until water has evaporated and rice is cooked through. Drain any excess water if necessary, but do not rinse. Remove bay and curry leaves. Place the rice in a large shallow dish, set aside uncovered, and allow rice to cool completely. Fluff the rice grains with a fork. To serve, place equal amounts of the rice into bowls and add 4 egg quarters per bowl. Divide the smoked trout and place on top of the rice. Sprinkle with parsley, pepper and serve with lemon wedges.

CHOOK'S TIPS

Placing the spices in the rice during cooking allows all the flavour to permeate through the rice. This is my shortcut method to maximize great flavour. Substitute smoked trout with smoked salmon, tinned tuna or even a piece of freshly grilled tuna.

In the event you'd like to try poaching fish, it's not difficult; just place 2 cups of milk and 2 cups of water and the dried leaves into a medium saucepan and bring to a gentle simmer. Turn heat to low and add some smoked fish. Simmer until fish starts to flake, around 8 minutes. Remove fish from the liquid, discard skin and any bones and set aside until required. Reserve 1 cup of strained poaching liquid in case you need to add moisture to the rice.

Breads

Breads

Bacon & Egg Cupcakes

Savoury cupcakes are so cute. And these Bacon & Egg cupcakes are the bomb – great looking little treats that add wow factor to any gathering! They are surprisingly easy to make, in a few short stages, and they're certain to top the party list.

Ingredients – makes 12

30g softened butter, for greasing

6 slices streaky **bacon**, cut into 2cm pieces

2 - 3 tablespoons of maple syrup

1 tablespoon vegetable oil

2 tablespoons onion confit (cooked, caramelised onion)

1½ cups self-raising flour

1 teaspoon baking powder

Sea salt and freshly ground black pepper

1 cup tasty cheese, grated

1 cup diced, cooked bacon

40g melted butter

2 tablespoons additional maple syrup

4 large **eggs**

1 cup buttermilk

Egg Mousse

6 extra-large **eggs**

½ cup onion confit (cooked, caramelised onion)

1 teaspoon hot English mustard, depending on taste

2 - 3 tablespoons thickened cream

2 - 3 tablespoons whole **egg** mayonnaise

Sea salt and freshly ground black pepper

To assemble:

Allow cupcakes to cool to room temperature. Pipe egg mousse over the top of the cupcakes and top with a piece of reserved caramelised bacon. Cupcakes are best served on the day of baking.

Method

Caramelised Bacon Garnish:

Preheat oven to 200°C. Line a baking sheet with baking paper.

Place bacon pieces 1cm apart. Brush both sides of the bacon with 2 tablespoons of the maple syrup and bake for 12 - 15 minutes or until cooked and caramelised. Remove from the oven and allow to cool.

Egg Mousse:

Place all the ingredients in a small food processor, (starting with 2 tablespoons of both the thickened cream and mayonnaise), and pulse until combined. Scrape down the sides and pulse for another few seconds until the mousse is thick and smooth. Check consistency at this stage, as mousse needs to be squeezable from a piping bag, yet still hold shape when piped onto the cupcakes. Add a small amount of additional cream and mayonnaise if you need to loosen the mixture. Place egg mix into a pastry bag fitted with a star nozzle. Refrigerate until required.

Bacon Cupcakes:

Lightly grease a 12 hole muffin tray with the softened butter. Preheat oven to 180°C. Sift flours, salt and pepper into a large bowl. Add grated cheese, cooked bacon and onion confit and thoroughly combine. In a medium bowl, combine the butter, additional maple syrup, eggs and buttermilk. Pour the egg mix into the flour and cheese mix, and stir to just combine. Don't over mix. Divide batter into the muffin tray. Bake for approximately 20 - 25 minutes until browned, or until a skewer inserted comes out clean.

CHOOK'S TIPS

Cupcakes without the mousse topping can be warmed slightly in a microwave for a few seconds. Caramelised bacon and egg mousse can be made the day before. For my vegetarian friends, sun-dried tomatoes and capers work well here instead of bacon, but then, they won't quite be Bacon Cupcakes.

Breads

Spicy Salami & Bacon Bread

This delectable loaf is an accidental creation that evolved while trying to make bacon scones. I didn't have quite enough bacon, so I substituted with some salami and added a whole lot of grated parmesan to the mixture. The scones turned out pretty good, so I made it again in a loaf tin and here's the result. Quick and easy to prepare, my spicy salami and bacon loaf is deliciously moist and packed full of flavour.

Ingredients – makes one loaf

30g softened butter, for greasing
2 cups self-raising flour
1 teaspoon baking powder
½ cup grated parmesan cheese
½ teaspoon each of sea salt and freshly ground black pepper
¼ teaspoon cayenne pepper
2 large fresh **eggs**, lightly beaten
1¾ cups buttermilk
1 garlic clove, finely minced
125g rindless short-cut **bacon**, finely chopped
125g spicy **salami**, finely chopped or **wurst**
2 tablespoons sun dried tomatoes, coarsely chopped
1/3 cup green olives stuffed with anchovies, halved
Extra grated parmesan cheese for sprinkling

Method

Preheat oven to 180°C. Grease a 24 x 13 x 7cm loaf tin with butter and line with baking paper. Sift the flour, baking powder, parmesan, salt and peppers into a large mixing bowl. In a separate small bowl, combine the eggs, garlic and buttermilk. Pour the wet ingredients into the dry ingredients and stir to combine, but don't over mix. If the batter appears too dry, you can adjust with another tablespoon or so of buttermilk. Add the bacon, salami, sun-dried tomatoes and olives and gently stir until combined. Pour mixture into baking tin. Sprinkle with extra parmesan and bake for 35 - 40 minutes until golden brown and cooked through, or until a skewer inserted comes out clean. Leave the bread to rest in the tin for 5 minutes before turning out and serving.

CHOOK'S TIPS

If the top of the loaf browns too quickly during cooking, loosely cover with foil. Try this recipe in a vegetarian version by substituting the bacon and salami with additional chopped sun dried tomatoes and olives. This bread is irresistible served straight from the oven or at room temperature. It does keep well in the fridge and on the second day, toast it up and serve with eggs and some home-made chutney. It's a great loaf to serve on an antipasto platter or take along to a picnic.

Breads

Florentine Brunch Baguettes

'Florentine' usually refers to a meal served on a bed of spinach, or with spinach in the recipe. This version epitomizes the flavours without compromising the integrity of 'Eggs Florentine'. Great as a portable snack for picnics, school lunches, or for a quick throw together when unexpected guests arrive.

Ingredients – serves 4

2 cups **bacon**, finely diced, cooked and drained

1 large baguette

6 hard-boiled **eggs**, quartered

1 cup prepared creamed spinach

1 cup prepared **hollandaise** sauce (optional)

Method

Cut the baguette in half lengthways. Remove some of the soft 'fluffy' bread from inside and reserve for another use. Fill the baguette with the bacon, top with warmed creamed spinach and the eggs and drizzle a little hollandaise sauce over, if using. Place the top of the baguette over the prepared half, cut into quarters and serve.

CHOOK'S TIPS

You can use tinned tuna or cooked, diced chicken instead of the bacon, if you prefer. Just as easy to prepare and just as delicious. Use the reserved bread to make fresh breadcrumbs for a meatloaf or rissoles.

Soups

Soups

Congee (Chinese Rice Soup)

If it wasn't for my house students, I doubt I would ever have made this meal. It is one of their all-time favourites and the possibilities with congee are as broad as with risottos and omelettes. Congee is comforting and moreish. You'll love this version.

Ingredients – serves 4

1 tablespoon sesame seeds

1 tablespoon peanut oil

2 Asian shallots, or 1 medium brown onion, finely chopped

8 rindless **bacon** rashers, diced or equal quantity of lap cheung Chinese **sausage**, sliced, approximately 400g

1 cup Japanese sushi rice or other short grain rice

4 cups strong flavoured chicken stock plus 2 - 3 cups water

2 cloves garlic, minced

½ teaspoon sesame oil

1 teaspoon fresh ginger, minced

1 - 2 tablespoons Japanese soy

White pepper, to season

4 large fresh **eggs** or 8 quail **eggs**, either fried or boiled, to serve

2 spring onions, finely sliced on the diagonal, for garnish

Method

In a small frying pan, dry-fry the sesame seeds over medium - high heat, until they start to brown and become fragrant, about 1 - 2 minutes. Remove from the frying pan and set aside. Heat the peanut oil in a large saucepan over medium - high heat. Add the shallots or onions and the bacon or lap cheung and cook until the onion is soft and the meat is browned, about 5 minutes for bacon and 8 minutes if using lap cheung. Remove onion and meat mix from the saucepan and set aside, leaving any residual oils in the saucepan. Turn the heat to high and add the rice to the saucepan, stirring well to coat all the grains. When the rice starts to crackle, add one cup of chicken stock. Stir gently until the liquid evaporates. Add another cup of stock, garlic, sesame oil and ginger and stir through. Turn the heat down to very low. Continue adding the remaining chicken stock and water, 1 cup at a time, at each interval once the liquid has almost evaporated. Add soy and pepper to taste and adjust seasoning as required. Continue cooking for at least another 40 minutes over a very low heat, stirring occasionally to make sure the rice doesn't stick to the bottom.

After 40 minutes, stir through the onion and meat mix and continue cooking for a further 10 minutes, allowing flavours to infuse. Top with additional stock or water as required during the entire cooking process. Congee needs to remain wet, thick and glossy but not gluggy. Once the rice has reached a wet porridge-like consistency, (individual grains of rice will have broken down and soup will appear starchy), remove the saucepan from the heat. Serve in bowls, topped with eggs and garnished with spring onions and a sprinkle of reserved sesame seeds.

CHOOK'S TIPS

Making congee is fairly similar to making a risotto, although the cooking process is very slow and takes much longer. Congee soup is thick and starchy. Stirring regularly and cooking for a long slow period releases the starch and thickens the soup. Risotto 'purists' prefer to keep the integrity of each rice grain intact, so not as much stirring is required, especially in the initial stages of cooking. Substitute the lap cheung for barbecue pork for another Asian flavour variation, or even some chopped chicken. You shouldn't need to add salt as the bacon, lap cheung and soy contain plenty. Lap cheung is a very sweet Chinese sausage and is available in Asian grocery stores or Asian butchers. Traditionally Asian based flavours are used for Congee, although I've done this with a tomato-based stock using chicken as the protein, and also with a coconut milk and laksa paste as the base and prawns as the hero of the dish.

Soups

Stracciatella

Stracciatella is an Italian egg and spinach soup, which is usually prepared without the bacon, but you'll find it is a wonderful addition to this delicious, hearty Mediterranean soup.

Ingredients – serves 4

1 – 2 tablespoons extra virgin olive oil
6 rindless **bacon** rashers, roughly chopped
6 cups strong flavoured chicken stock
6 large silver beet leaves, washed, dried thoroughly, coarsely chopped
1 tablespoon onion confit (cooked, caramelised onion)
2 spring onions, sliced finely on the diagonal, green tips reserved for garnish
Freshly ground black pepper
3 large **eggs**, beaten
½ cup flat leaf parsley, chopped
Parmesan cheese, freshly grated, for garnish

Method

Heat 1 teaspoon of the oil in a large saucepan over medium heat and cook the bacon until browned and crispy. Drain on paper towels and set aside. Wipe saucepan clean, add the stock and bring to the boil. Add spinach, cooked onion, reserved bacon and spring onion whites and reduce heat to low, simmering for 2 - 3 minutes. Season with pepper. Just before serving, hold a small-holed strainer over the saucepan. Drizzle the beaten egg into the strainer allowing the egg to drop into the soup. The eggs will set straight away, like little strings. Turn off the heat. Serve immediately, garnished with reserved spring onion tips, parsley, parmesan cheese and a drizzle of remaining oil in each bowl.

CHOOK'S TIPS

This soup is also great with finely chopped prosciutto or chopped cooked chicken meat. Vegetarians can substitute the chicken stock for vegetable stock and leave out the bacon. You won't need to season with a lot of salt, as both parmesan and bacon contain sufficient amounts.

87

Soups

Salmorejo

Salmorejo is a cold Spanish soup with bacon and egg 'croutons'. It makes a fantastic starter and is a taste sensation. Although salmorejo is traditionally served cold, warming it slightly will enhance the depth of flavour. If you like gazpacho, you'll really like this one.

Ingredients – serves 4-6

4 slices sourdough bread, crusts removed
2 cups water
750g ripe Roma tomatoes
250g tinned chopped tomatoes, including juice
½ cup prepared onion confit (cooked, caramelised onion)
3 cloves garlic, minced
1/3 cup extra virgin olive oil, plus extra for drizzling
2 - 3 tablespoons fresh lemon juice
½ teaspoon brown sugar (optional)
Sea salt and freshly ground black pepper
6 hard-boiled **eggs**, roughly chopped
6 rindless **bacon** rashers, finely chopped, fried until crisp, drained
Croutons for garnish (optional)

Method

Place bread into the water and soften. Squeeze out the water by hand and set bread aside. Bring a medium saucepan of water to the boil. With a sharp knife, make a small cross slit at the base and top of each tomato. Gently lower the tomatoes into the boiling water for 45 - 60 seconds, or just until skins start to come away from the flesh. Using tongs, remove tomatoes and plunge them into a bowl of iced water. This will stop the cooking process. When cool enough to handle, remove and discard the tomato skins, seeds and core and roughly chop. Place the bread, chopped Roma and tinned tomatoes, onion confit, garlic, olive oil, lemon juice and sugar, if using, into a blender and puree until smooth. Season to taste and refrigerate until chilled. Divide the egg and bacon into serving dishes, leaving a little of each for garnish. Pour thickened soup over the egg and bacon. Top with remaining chopped egg and bacon, and croutons if using. Drizzle with some additional olive oil just before serving.

 **CHOOK'S TIPS**

You can adjust the quantities to turn this tomato soup base into a thickened dressing to drizzle over bacon & eggs on toast, or as a fresh pasta sauce. This soup keeps well for 3 days, refrigerated in an airtight container. Salmorejo is great without bacon too. Substitute the meat for 1 cup finely grated parmesan and, my vegetarian friends, you're on a winner!

Soups

Smokey Bacon Stock

The basis to every great soup starts with a great stock and my smokey bacon stock is no exception. To ensure you get it right every time, follow the steps as shown here, using the best ingredients available, and you'll have a great platform for a multitude of wonderful recipes.

Ingredients - makes 3 litres

750g **ham hock**, double smoked

750g **smoked ribs**, chopped

2 large parsnips, peeled and chopped into large pieces

1 large swede, peeled and quartered

3 large ribs celery, halved width ways

4 large carrots, peeled and halved

1 large brown onion, peeled and left whole

8 sprigs flat leaf parsley

1 teaspoon whole black pepper corns

 CHOOK'S TIPS

Salt is not needed for this stock, as the smoked hock, smoked ribs or any other bacon bones or smoked meats you may choose will contain plenty. This stock has incredible intensity of flavour, so remember a little bit goes a long way. I always boil smoked bones initially for a few minutes only, and then refresh with clean water, as I feel this removes a lot of the salt content that's used in the process of curing. This step is optional though. Stock freezes well for up to 3 months. It's perfect for use in pea and ham soup, potato and sausage soup, Hungarian bean soup, or any other hearty dish requiring a smokey stock base. It's also great to use in roasts and risottos. Double smoked ham hocks and smoked ribs are available from selected continental delicatessens. A great tip is to ask your butcher to cut the hock into 4 pieces. Marrow always adds extra flavour.

Method

Place hock and ribs in a large stock pot and cover with water. Bring to the boil and cook uncovered for 2 minutes, then discard water, leaving the meat bones in the pot. Add the vegetables and peppercorns to the pot, and cover with fresh water to come 2cm above the ingredients. Bring to the boil, reduce heat to low, and remove any scum that comes to the surface. Simmer for at least 4 hours. As water levels drop below the level of the ingredients, top up with water as required, so that the ingredients are always just submerged by approximately 2cm. After 4 hours, turn off heat and remove the meat and bones from the soup. When cool enough to handle, separate the meat from the bones, discarding any fat or sinew. Shred the meat, and place into a clean airtight container, and refrigerate until ready to use.

Reheat the stove to low, place bones back into the stock and continue to simmer the bones and vegetables for a further 2 hours, continually topping water levels as required. After simmering for 6 hours in total, the stock should be rich in colour and the flavour should be intensely smokey. Remove and discard all the vegetables and bones and strain the stock, leaving the liquid to cool. Refrigerate overnight. Discard the layer of fat from the stock surface and store in airtight containers until required.

Soups

Bacon & Egg Soup

Yes, that's right, bacon & egg soup! A warming, flavoursome, clear broth soup, with all the goodies — bite size pieces of tantalizing bacon, crunchy epi seed baguette, and topped with a soft poached egg — simply heaven in a bowl. Bacon & egg soup can be eaten at any time, and especially for breakfast or brunch on a cold winter's day.

Ingredients - serves 4

4 slices per bowl of epi-seeded bread
Extra virgin olive oil, for drizzling
6 cups chicken stock
2 cups smoky bacon stock - see previous recipe
4 rindless **bacon** rashers, fried until crisp, drained and chopped
½ cup parsley, finely chopped
4 large poached **eggs**, for serving

Method

Bread:

Lightly brush the bread with olive oil and bake in the oven for 4 minutes until crunchy. Prepare the poached eggs and set aside.

Soup:

Bring the chicken and bacon stocks to the boil and ladle 2 cups into each serving bowl. Divide the bread, bacon & parsley into bowls, top with a poached egg in each bowl and serve immediately.

 CHOOK'S TIPS

Any crunchy bread can be used in place of the epi-seeded baguette. If you don't have bacon stock, you can use chicken stock. The bacon stock adds a mild smoky taste which enhances the flavour for this wonderful bacon and egg soup.

Quiches, Pies and Tarts

Serving up a home-made pie or quiche shouldn't be reserved for special occasions. For me, it's always been an enjoyable experience as I get to be creative.

Similar to making risottos and soups, your quiche, pie or tart is a blank canvas. You design your masterpiece using fabulous produce, from simple three ingredient tarts to complex structures like a timpano pie. Whatever you create will be a satisfying meal for family and friends.

My darling mum Lorraine never attempted to make quiches or pies. She says she could never be bothered with all the fuss that goes with making pastry. And in mum's day, the ready-made pastry or pre-baked pastry cases were not readily available as they are now.

So, there's no need to worry if you can't be bothered making your own pastry. All supermarkets stock ready-made puff, filo and short crust pastries, making cooking much simpler, so get cracking and have fun.

Quiches, Pies and Tarts

Quiche Lorraine

Quiche Lorraine is a classic dish, eaten for brunch, lunch, or even a light dinner, served with a fresh garden salad. The secret to achieving the authentic, assertive flavours for the perfect quiche lorraine is most certainly the gruyere cheese and a melt-in-your-mouth buttery short crust pastry.

Ingredients – serves 4-6

1¾ cups plain flour

150g butter, chilled and chopped into 2cm cubes

1 large fresh **egg yolk**, reserve **egg white**

3 - 4 tablespoons cold water, or a little more if needed

250g cooked **bacon** or **ham**, finely diced

4 large fresh **eggs**, beaten

¼ teaspoon nutmeg

350ml thickened cream

100ml buttermilk

75g gruyere cheese, grated

Freshly ground black pepper

CHOOK'S TIPS

Many quiche lorraine recipes I've tried contain mustard, cooked onions or even spring onions. You can experiment by adding various condiments to develop flavours. For a vegetarian version, just leave out the bacon or ham and add cooked, chopped spinach or blanched asparagus and green beans. It won't be a quiche lorraine in the traditional sense, but it will be tasty. As a short cut, you can use 1 - 2 sheets puff pastry, just thawed, or a store bought prepared pie crust. I've also used filo pastry and made individual filo pies for party food and picnics (as shown in this photo). For me, the buttermilk mellows out the saltiness of the bacon in taste. If you don't have buttermilk, you can substitute with extra cream.

Method

Pastry:

In a food processor, combine the flour and butter until the mixture resembles fine breadcrumbs. Then pulse in the egg yolk and enough of the water to just bring the dough together to a pliable consistency. Roll into a ball, flatten slightly and cover with plastic food wrap. Refrigerate for 20 minutes. Preheat the oven to 180°C. Roll out the pastry on a lightly floured surface and carefully place the pastry into a 23cm round baking dish, preferably a tart tin with removable base. Prick the pastry gently all over with a fork and freeze for 10 minutes. Blind bake the pastry case for 15 minutes. Allow to cool for 10 minutes before adding the filling.

Filling:

Scatter the cooked bacon or ham evenly in the pastry case. Combine the eggs, reserved egg white, nutmeg, cream and buttermilk. Pour the egg mix over the bacon and sprinkle with cheese and black pepper. Bake for approximately 25 - 30 minutes or until puffed, golden and cooked through. Serve warm or at room temperature.

97

Quiches, Pies and Tarts

Bacon, Feta & Egg Tart

There's nothing quite like the wafting aroma of a pie or tart baking in the oven. Crispy puff pastry and soft savoury custard centre, punctuated with tasty little bacon pieces. Here's a lovely tart for you to try....

Ingredients – serves 8

2 sheets puff pastry, just thawed

8 rindless streaky **bacon** rashers, sliced very thin

30g softened butter, for greasing

4 fresh **eggs**, lightly beaten

¼ cup parmesan cheese, freshly grated

½ cup cream

Freshly ground black pepper

100g feta cheese, crumbled

1 tablespoon chives, finely chopped

4 large fresh **egg yolks** (optional)

Method

Preheat oven to 200°C. Remove pastry from freezer. Roll the streaky bacon into cylindrical tubes and secure with toothpicks. Place on a small baking tray and cook for approximately 10 - 12 minutes or until the fat starts to render. Remove from the oven and leave to cool on oven tray. They will firm up in this time. Reduce oven temperature to 180°C. Grease a 35 x 25 x 2cm baking tray with butter. Place the pastry in the tray, trimming any extra overhanging pieces. You'll only need just over half the second sheet. Gently push the pastry edges up the side of the tray, then align and press both pieces together to seal the base. Prick the pastry all over with a fork. Combine the eggs, parmesan, cream and pepper. Crumble the feta over the pastry. Carefully remove toothpicks from the bacon and arrange the bacon onto the pastry. Gently pour the egg mix over the pastry. Sprinkle with chives and bake for 20 - 25 minutes, or until egg custard is set and pastry is crisp and golden.

CHOOK'S TIPS

Salt is not required for this tart, as the bacon and feta contain plenty. As a vegetarian version, omit the bacon and use a selection of your favourite vegetables: lightly sautéed leeks, baby spinach leaves, roasted eggplant, thinly sliced button mushrooms, and soft herbs such as parsley or chervil are also great. In the photo shown here, I have arranged the bacon into cylindrical shapes and carefully placed 4 egg yolks into the mixture just before baking. Bacon cylinders are fiddly, but you can use the feta chunks to prop them up and hold them in place. Thinner pieces of bacon are more pliable and hold their shape better when making cylinders. Ask your butcher to slice the bacon very thin; you may need to give them some notice for this order.

Quiches, Pies and Tarts

Garlic Baguette & Butter Pudding

Savoury puddings are wonderful and are a great accompaniment to any meal. This is my savoury take on the old fashioned bread and butter pudding. Use day old baguettes, so there's lots of crunchy topping to go around.

Ingredients - serves 8

4 rindless **bacon** rashers cut into 5cm pieces

½ cup softened butter, approximately 120g

3 large cloves garlic, minced

2 large fresh **eggs**

1 cup milk

½ cup thickened cream

1 tablespoon prepared onion confit (cooked, caramelised onion), or 2 teaspoons French onion soup mix

Freshly ground black pepper and a pinch of sea salt

1 large baguette, sliced width ways to 2cm pieces (don't cut all the way to the base)

 CHOOK'S TIPS

Danish or Hungarian salami slices are also a delicious alternative to the bacon. This is easily adapted to a vegetarian version, substitute the bacon with slices of portobello mushrooms or thick tomato slices.

Method

In a large frying pan, lightly brown the bacon on both sides until the fat starts to render. Remove and drain on paper towels.

Garlic Butter:

Combine the garlic and butter. Set aside until required. In a medium sized bowl, beat the eggs, milk, cream, onion confit or onion soup mix and season as required.

To Assemble

Preheat oven to 180°C. Lightly grease a 32 x 16 x 5cm baking dish. Butter the baguette slices liberally on both sides and on top with the garlic butter and arrange them standing upright in the baking dish. Place a piece of bacon between each slice and around the edges of the dish. Pour the mixture to three quarters of the way up the bread. Refrigerate for at least an hour before cooking. This will allow the bread to absorb the egg and milk mixture. Bake for 25 - 30 minutes or until the egg custard is cooked through, and the crust is crunchy and golden. Custard should be a little bit wobbly but not runny. Serve warm.

Mains

Mains

Frittata with Bacon & Peas

Frittatas, like omelettes, have endless possibilities. Delectable and comforting, they can be as simple or as sophisticated as you like. These thick Italian omelettes are great for breakfast, al fresco lunch, or an anytime meal; they're filling, nutritious and best of all, kids love them too.

Ingredients – serves 2-3

6 large fresh **eggs**, beaten
6 rindless short-cut **bacon** rashers, diced
¾ cup frozen peas
½ teaspoon dried Italian herbs
1 tablespoon thickened cream
Freshly ground black pepper
2 tablespoons olive oil
½ cup of parmesan cheese, freshly grated (optional)
Fresh small basil leaves for garnish

CHOOK'S TIPS

Alternate frittata fillings can be mushrooms, cooked and peeled broad beans, smoked salmon and dill, or any other favourite ingredients. I sometimes add 1 tablespoon of onion confit (cooked, caramelised onions) to the mixture for extra flavor.

Method

Pre-heat the grill to medium. Combine all ingredients except the olive oil, parmesan and basil leaves. In a medium frying pan, heat 1 tablespoon of the oil over medium - high heat. Pour in the contents all at once. Turn heat down to low. Allow the egg to just set. Tilt the frying pan and allow the uncooked egg to run underneath.

Set frying pan back on the heat for 30 seconds. Tilt the pan again, allowing more of the uncooked egg to flow underneath and continue to cook the eggs until almost set. Sprinkle the parmesan cheese over the frittata and place the frying pan under the grill. When the omelette is completely set and cheese is melted, slide the frittata onto a prepared plate, garnish with the basil leaves and serve immediately. Alternatively, allow frittata to cool to room temperature, cut into small squares and serve.

Note: I've cooked my frittatas here in individual 10cm diameter cast iron frying pans, which are available in kitchen equipment stores. Preheat the oven to 180°C. Grease the base and sides of the frying pans with the oil. Combine the remaining ingredients and half the parmesan cheese. Divide equal amounts of the egg mix into the individual frying pans, sprinkle with remaining parmesan on top and bake in the oven for 25 minutes or until puffed and cooked through.

Mains

Sticky Pork Spare Ribs

I tried these pork ribs at a friend's barbecue many years ago. The ribs were browned on the barbecue first and then baked in the oven. The creator was very guarded with the recipe, so I gave it a whirl myself. Voila!

Ingredients – makes 8 full size portions or 16 cocktail size portions

¼ cup Japanese soy sauce

2 tablespoons dark soy sauce

1 tablespoon garlic, minced

1 tablespoon ginger, minced

¼ cup runny honey

1 teaspoon dark brown sugar

1 star anise seed

Pinch of ground cinnamon

1 teaspoon sesame oil

2 teaspoon peanut oil

8 **pork spare ribs**, 3cm thickness, tuff outer rind removed

 **CHOOK'S TIPS**

Beef and chicken can be substituted for the pork spare ribs, although cooking times will vary.

Method

Place the ribs in a large bowl. Combine the soy sauces, garlic, ginger, honey, sugar, star anise, cinnamon, sesame oil, and 1 teaspoon peanut oil to make a marinade and pour over the ribs. Cover and marinate for at least 2 hours, turning once. Drain the marinade and reserve for later use.

Preheat oven to 180°C. Heat the oil in a large heavy based frying pan over a medium - high heat. Place the spare ribs in the pan, fat side down, and cook for 6 - 7 minutes until fat starts to render and crisp up nicely. You can cook for a few minutes longer if you want a really crunchy top. Then turn the pieces on their sides and brown all other sides for a further 2 minutes each.

Place the ribs in a small baking dish so they all fit snugly, ensuring the crispy side is facing up. Pour enough of the reserved marinade over the ribs to come a third of the way up the height of the ribs. Cover loosely with foil. Turn oven down to 150°C and bake for approximately 45 minutes. Remove the foil and baste the ribs all over with marinade. If the sauce is really thick, you can add a small amount of water to loosen it. Continue baking for a further 45 minutes, uncovered, until cooked through and sauce has reduced and thickened. Serve with boiled rice or cooked Korean potato noodles and Asian greens.

Mains

Pork Schnitzels with Sauce Gribiche & Rainbow Slaw

Friday nights at my grandmother's house were always a feast. It was either baked chicken or schnitzels. Nan used veal for her schnitzels. I watched the procedure with hawk eyes, and sometimes I was allowed to do the flour, egg and crumb coating if she didn't have things under control, which wasn't that often.

Ingredients – pork schnitzels – serve 2 as main

Sauce Gribiche

6 large hard-boiled **eggs**

3 hard-boiled **egg yolks**

½ cup whole **egg mayonnaise**

2 teaspoons capers, finely chopped

1 large pickled cucumber, finely chopped

½ teaspoon lemon zest

1 tablespoon parsley, finely chopped

Rainbow Slaw

¼ red cabbage, finely sliced

1 carrot, finely grated

1 stick celery, finely sliced

1 spring onion, finely sliced

Sea salt and white pepper, to season

Schnitzels

2 large **pork** schnitzels

Plain flour, for coating (approximately 1 cup)

2 **eggs**, lightly beaten

1 - 1½ cups Japanese panko breadcrumbs, or plain breadcrumbs

Vegetable oil for frying

Lemon slices for garnish

Method

Sauce Gribiche:

Mix all the ingredients until well combined. Cover and set aside until required.

Rainbow Slaw:

Combine all the ingredients, and season with sea salt and white pepper.

Schnitzels:

Place the flour, egg and breadcrumbs in 3 separate bowls. Coat the schnitzels in the flour and pat down to ensure even coverage. Dip the schnitzels in egg and then coat in the breadcrumbs. Heat the oil in a large frying pan over medium to high heat. Oil should be hot enough so when a small cube of bread is dropped into the oil, it browns in 30 seconds. Turn heat down to medium and cook the schnitzels for about 2 - 2½ minutes on each side. Drain on paper towels. Serve schnitzels with Sauce Gribiche, Rainbow Slaw and garnish with lemon slices.

 **CHOOK'S TIPS**

Add some onion powder to the flour at the coating stage for a more robust flavour. I don't add anything to the slaw, as the Gribiche is quite rich and 'wets' the salad well enough.

Mains

Greek Baked Pork Chops – Alonissos style

My time spent living in Greece was invaluable. I learnt many skills and incredible flavour combinations from the neighbourly yayas (grandmothers) of Alonissos, whose sole purpose in life, as with many cultures, is to nourish their loved ones. One of the world's most delicious cuisines is so prevalent in this amazing dish.

Ingredients – serves 4

½ teaspoon each of cumin and coriander seeds

6 juniper berries, gently crushed

8 **pork** chops or **pork** cutlets

2 tablespoons Greek olive oil

4 bay leaves

1 cinnamon stick

4 sprigs fresh thyme, leaves picked

3 garlic cloves, minced

1 teaspoon dried Greek oregano, or more if required

1 large brown onion, peeled and roughly chopped

400g tinned tomatoes, or 1½ cups home-made tomato passata

Zest and juice of 1 lemon

1 teaspoon brown sugar

1½ cups strong flavoured chicken stock

Sea salt and freshly ground black pepper

8 large fresh **eggs**

Method

Pre-heat the oven to 180°C. In a large frying pan over high heat, dry-fry the cumin and coriander seeds and the juniper berries, shaking the pan regularly, for a minute or so or until they become fragrant. Allow to cool and grind in a spice grinder or in a mortar and pestle. Heat 1 teaspoon of the oil in the same frying pan over medium - high heat and sear the cutlets until well browned on both sides and any fat is rendered along the edges. Place cutlets into a large, deep 40 x 30cm baking dish and set aside. Sprinkle the spice mix over the chops and add the bay leaves, cinnamon stick, thyme, garlic, oregano, onion, tomatoes, zest and lemon juice, sugar and chicken stock. Season as required and tightly cover the chops with foil. Reduce oven temperature to 150°C and bake for 2 hours.

After 2 hours, discard the foil and cinnamon stick and increase the heat to 180°C. Crack eggs into pockets of sauce between the chops and return the baking dish to the oven. Cook for a further 15 - 20 minutes or until the sauce reduces and the eggs are cooked to your liking.

 CHOOK'S TIPS

When you remove the foil, you may have a lot of stock. If you feel there's too much stock, remove some of it before adding the eggs. Don't discard the extra stock as it can be frozen and used at a later stage as a great base stock for soups or casseroles. For a really hearty meal, add peeled chopped potatoes to the baking dish with the cutlets. The potatoes will break down and thicken up the gravy. Vegetarians will be happy to know that this meal can be made substituting the pork for thick slices of eggplant and zucchinis sliced in half horizontally. Lightly brown the eggplant the same way as the pork cutlets; add potatoes and bake for 1½ hours. This meal is also wonderful with chicken or a meaty fish such as swordfish. Cooking times will vary for the chicken and fish. Greek olive oil is available in most continental delicatessens.

Mains

Russian Cabbage Rolls

Pork, veal and beef mince with cabbage are very popular in Eastern Europe and together they create a multitude of delicious meals from soups to mains. There are many variations of cabbage rolls, and this is an adaptation of a recipe my grandmother gave me. I've included pork mince for the purpose of this book, although my Nan would have used only veal or beef.

Ingredients – makes approximately 24

1 large white cabbage

400g **pork** mince

400g beef mince

1½ cups white rice, partially cooked and cooled

1 large **egg** or 2 small **eggs**

1 large brown onion, finely chopped

¼ cup dill, finely chopped

2 teaspoons sweet paprika

¼ teaspoons caraway seeds

Sea salt and freshly ground black pepper

1½ cups strong beef stock, or 2 beef stock cubes diluted in 1½ cups water

1 cup chicken stock

400g tinned, chopped tomatoes

¼ teaspoon sugar

Fresh flat leaf parsley or fresh sprigs of dill for garnish

Method

Cut the cabbage in half and remove the tough ribs. Soften the leaves in boiling water for a few minutes, refresh in ice water, drain and pat off excess water. Thoroughly combine the pork and beef mince, rice, egg, onion, dill, paprika, caraway seeds, salt and pepper. Take small portions of meat mixture, about the size of 1 - 2 tablespoons, accommodating each leaf size, and roll into sausage shapes. Lay one cabbage leaf on a board. Starting at the base core end of the leaf, gently wrap each leaf around the sausage, tucking in sides as you roll.

Place each roll into a large baking dish side by side. If there is extra meat left over, it can be rolled into balls and baked separately in another smaller dish in some stock. Preheat oven to 180°C. Combine both of the stocks, tomatoes and sugar. Pour stock over the cabbage rolls, to come half way up the sides of the rolls. Season as required and cover tightly with foil. Reduce oven temperature to 170°C and bake for 1½ hours.

CHOOK'S TIPS

Cabbage rolls freeze really well, but make sure you add some of the cooking stock to the container when freezing. Serve cabbage rolls on their own, or with pasta or boiled potatoes. Chicken or veal mince are also great alternatives to pork and beef.

Mains

Spanakopita (Spinach, Feta & Bacon Pie)

Another traditional specialty from Greece - the almighty Spinach Pie. I could eat this every day and the truth be known, I did eat it almost every day when I lived in Greece. Bacon isn't usually an ingredient found in Spanakopita, but it's a great addition in this pie.

Ingredients - serves 8

1 packet filo pastry
30g softened butter, for greasing
1 large bunch spinach or silver beet, stems discarded and leaves roughly chopped
1½ cups cooked **bacon** or **ham**
200g feta
200g ricotta
5 large fresh **eggs**
1 small brown onion, finely diced
4 spring onions, chopped
1 teaspoon fresh dill, finely chopped (optional)
¼ teaspoon dried mint leaves (optional)
1/3 cup melted butter, or more if required
Freshly ground black pepper

 **CHOOK'S TIPS**

If the top layer of filo is browning too quickly, cover Spanakopita lightly with foil and continue baking. As an alternative, I have also made this pie with some chopped semi dried tomatoes in lieu of the bacon and it's really, really good.

Method

Take the filo from the fridge an hour before required. Preheat oven to 180°C. Grease a 30 x 20cm baking dish with softened butter. In a large mixing bowl, combine the spinach or silver beet, bacon or ham, feta, ricotta, eggs, onion, spring onion, and dill and mint, if using. Season with pepper and set aside. Working quickly, lay the filo pastry on a clean surface. Butter one sheet with the melted butter and line the baking dish.

Meanwhile, keep the other sheets covered with a clean, lightly dampened cloth, which will prevent pastry from drying out. Repeat with another 3 sheets to line the base of the dish. Pour the spinach mixture into the baking dish and continue layering the top of the pie with buttered filo sheets. You can use 4, 5 or 6 sheets on the top and the bottom, depending on how much pastry you enjoy. Trim off any extra pastry or tuck it all into the sides of the dish. Butter the top sheet and bake Spanakopita for around 35 - 40 minutes or until pastry is golden and the filling is cooked through.

Mains

'No Bun' Gourmet Burgers with Beetroot Cream

Knife and fork are required for this burger…. Simple, fresh and everything a great burger should be, just without the bread. Ham, pineapple and beetroot is a wonderful culinary marriage and in this burger, it's no exception.

Ingredients – Serves 2

2 beef patties, preferably home-made
1 tablespoon olive oil
4 slices leg **ham** or **prosciutto**
2 pineapple rings or 3 tablespoons crushed pineapple
4 slices haloumi cheese
4 slow roasted tomato halves
2 large fresh **eggs**
2 - 3 tablespoons beetroot cream – recipe to follow
Gourmet baby lettuce leaves, to serve

CHOOK'S TIPS

The ham or prosciutto can be pan-fried if required. Beetroot cream, made with either the cumin spice or the dried mint leaves, makes a great dip too. Serve it with vegetable sticks, along with the hummus and any other dips you have in mind for a party table.

Method

Beetroot cream:

Blend 200g of cooked beetroot and 1 tablespoon beetroot liquid in a small food processor until smooth. Pour into a small non-reactive mixing bowl. Add 1 - 2 tablespoons of softened mascarpone or cream cheese and ½ teaspoon of ground cumin, or ½ teaspoon of dried mint leaves, and season with sea salt and freshly ground black pepper. Combine well and set aside until required. Makes approximately 1 cup.

Burgers:

In a large frying pan, heat 1 teaspoon of the oil over medium – high heat and cook the beef patties on both sides until cooked through. Cover, set aside and keep warm until required. Wipe the frying pan clean. Heat another teaspoon of the oil and cook the haloumi until well browned on both sides. Set aside with the beef patties. Meanwhile in another frying pan, cook the eggs to your liking.

To serve:

Place the burgers onto plates. Top with ham or prosciutto, pineapple, Roma tomatoes and haloumi slices and finally, the eggs. Garnish with lettuce and drizzle with beetroot cream. Serve immediately.

Chook's Pantry

Like most people, I have a million things to do every day, so I find advance preparation makes things easier in the kitchen. If I have certain ingredients in place, I can be time-savvy and prepare meals a lot quicker than always starting from scratch.

- onion confit (caramelised onions)
- chicken stock
- slow roasted tomatoes
- tomato passata
- white sauce
- creamed spinach
- minced ginger and minced garlic

Chook's Pantry

Onion Confit

I use onion confit, or caramelised onions, in just about every recipe requiring the use of onions. When onions are cooked over a very low heat for long periods of time, the natural sugars in the onions caramelise, producing a thick, glossy onion mix which adds the most intense flavours to your dishes. Add caramelised onions to muffins, breads, pasta sauces, pizza, soups, casseroles, pies, quiches, omelettes or any savoury dish you believe will benefit from extra flavour.

Ingredients – makes approximately 2 cups

8 large brown onions
2 tablespoons light olive oil, or more if required
2 tablespoons butter, or more if required (optional)
½ teaspoon sea salt and freshly ground black pepper

Method

Peel and chop the onions to a small dice or thin slice. Heat the oil, and butter if using, in a large saucepan and cook the onions for at least 30 minutes over a very low heat, stirring frequently. The longer you cook the onions, the sweeter and more intense the flavour.

CHOOK'S TIPS

You can also use this method for Spanish onions, white onions, leeks and garlic.

Chook's Pantry

Chicken Stock

If I don't have home-made chicken stock in the house, I start to panic. Besides caramelised onions, chicken stock is probably the most multipurpose ingredient in my fridge, and there are always back-up bottles in the deep freezer. I've had some great chicken soup over the years, but there's something about my great grandmother's recipe that just warms me. So before any discussion about who makes the best chicken stock in the world, give this recipe a try.

Ingredients – makes 7-8 litres of stock

1 frozen boiler or free range chicken
2 chicken carcasses
300g chicken giblets
300g chicken necks
1 large brown onion, peeled, left whole
3 medium parsnips, peeled and chopped into thirds
4 large carrots, peeled and chopped into thirds
4 celery stalks, chopped into thirds
1 large swede, peeled and chopped into quarters
4 garlic cloves
2 tablespoons cooking salt, or more as required
1 tablespoon black peppercorns
½ small bunch parsley, flat leaf or curly

Method

In a large soup pot, bring 12 litres of water to the boil and add all the chicken ingredients, salt and peppercorns, and all the vegetables, except the parsley. Bring back to the boil again, and cook ingredients for 2 minutes. Reduce heat to low, and remove any scum that comes to the surface. Add the parsley and simmer for at least 4 hours. After 4 hours, remove the chicken and allow to cool. Cut the chicken into 8 pieces. Return the chicken pieces and any juices to the pot. Simmer for another hour. Top the pot with water as you need, so the ingredients are always just submerged. Check for seasoning and adjust as required. Strain the chicken and the vegetables in a colander. Allow stock to cool before storing in airtight containers and refrigerating or freezing.

CHOOK'S TIPS

The longer you leave the stock to simmer, the more intense the flavour. Boilers have always provided great flavour for a chicken stock. The chicken from the boiler is tougher than other chicken, so I tend to discard it after cooking. If you're using a free range chicken, remove the juicy white and brown meat and place only the carcass back in to the pot. Reserve the meat for making your chicken soup or any other dish you have in mind. If you're making a chicken soup from the stock, the soup carrots are always good to add, along with some cooked fine egg noodles, which can be found in any supermarket or delicatessen.

Ask your chicken supplier if they have any frozen chicken egg yolks, which also add good flavour to the stock (and good eating). They're hard to find these days but some independent chicken shops can obtain them for you.

Chook's Pantry

Slow Roasted Tomatoes

Two great time savers and handy fridge stand-bys are slow roasted tomatoes and home-made tomato passata sauce. Roasted tomatoes can be served as they are, on an antipasto platter, or blended to make delicious pasta sauces. They can be used in casseroles and risottos, or on top of pizzas. The list is endless. A bolognese sauce made with chopped, tinned tomatoes can be good, but the intensely rich flavours that slow roasting deliver are so much better.

Method

Ripe Roma Tomatoes:

Preheat oven to 150°C. Line a baking tray with baking paper or foil.

Cut the tomatoes in half lengthways and place on the tray, cut side up. Generously drizzle with extra virgin olive oil and sprinkle with sea salt. At this stage, you can also add freshly ground black pepper, and some dried herbs of choice such as oregano, thyme or basil. Place the tray in the oven, and lower the heat to 120°C. Cook for 90 minutes.

The tomatoes will have collapsed by this stage, although still holding their shape in the skins. You can serve the slow roasted tomatoes with any meal, or gently place tomato halves and their juices in an airtight container and refrigerate for up to 1 week. To use the tomatoes in sauces, soups and casseroles, remove the skins before blending and adding to any creation.

 CHOOK'S TIPS

This same method can be applied to slow roasting zucchinis, mushrooms, onions, garlic and capsicums. With capsicum, I like to firstly char-grill them over a flame using heat proof tongs, or under a high grill, turning regularly, until the skins turn black. Then place them on a lined baking tray and cook for 90 minutes in a 120°C oven. Skins and membranes are easily removed once cooled.

Chook's Pantry

Home-Made Tomato Passata

Ingredients – *makes approximately 3 cups*

8 - 10 large Roma tomatoes
2 - 3 tablespoons extra virgin olive oil
2 medium brown onions, finely chopped
2 large garlic cloves, minced
1 - 2 tablespoons tomato paste
1 teaspoon brown sugar
5 large basil leaves, finely chopped (optional)
Sea salt and freshly ground black pepper
1 cup home-made chicken or vegetable stock (optional)

Method

In a medium saucepan, heat the oil and gently cook the onions over a very low heat for 15 minutes, stirring regularly. Add the garlic and cook for a further 2 minutes. Set aside. In the meantime, bring another medium saucepan of water to the boil. With a sharp knife, make a small cross slit at the base and top of each tomato. Gently lower the tomatoes into the boiling water for 45 - 60 seconds, or just until skins start to come away from the flesh. Using tongs, remove tomatoes and plunge them into a bowl of iced water. This will stop the cooking process. When cool enough to handle, remove and discard the tomato skins, seeds and core and chop pulp finely. Return the cooked onion and garlic to a medium heat on the stove. Add the tomato pulp, tomato paste, sugar and basil, if using. Season with salt and pepper and continue cooking tomato passata for 10 minutes until tomatoes begin to collapse. At this stage, you will have a very rich, full flavoured sauce. If you are using stock, add it at this stage and cook for a further 15 minutes, or until the sauce reduces and thickens. Once cooked, you can puree the passata if you want a smoother consistency. Refrigerate in clean airtight jars. Tomato passata stores well for up to 1 week.

Chook's Pantry

Creamed Spinach

Creamed spinach is another of my "must haves" and I make it often. It has a multitude of uses — as a base for soups, as a sauce for fish, veal, chicken, steak, and pork, and it makes a great topping for jacket potatoes, or even stirred through some pasta. It's a great way to get kids to eat their greens — they really love it.

Ingredients
– makes approximately 500mls

1 large brown onion or 1/3 cup prepared onion confit (cooked, caramelised onions)

2 teaspoons light olive oil

1 tablespoon of butter

750g frozen spinach thawed, or 5 bunches fresh English spinach, ends trimmed and finely chopped

1 cup chicken stock

1 cup prepared white sauce

3 large garlic cloves, minced

1 tablespoon thickened cream (optional)

Sea salt & freshly ground black pepper

Method

Peel and chop the onion to a small dice. Heat the oil and butter in a large saucepan and cook the onions for 30 minutes over a very low heat, stirring frequently. If using onion confit, you can skip this step. Turn heat up to medium. Add the stock and spinach and simmer for 8 - 10 minutes until cooked, stirring regularly. Add the white sauce, and cream if using, and combine thoroughly. Season to taste and stir regularly until the sauce thickens. Use additional chicken stock or water if the sauce becomes too thick. Once cooked, you can puree the spinach if you want a smoother consistency. Refrigerate in clean airtight jars. Creamed spinach stores well for up to 5 days.

 **CHOOK'S TIPS**

Creamed spinach is a delicious base for a great soup. Add approximately 2 cups of stock to every cup of creamed spinach, according to the desired consistency. Add some cooked diced chicken, or leftover lamb and croutons for a really hearty soup. Vegetable stock can be substituted for chicken stock.

Chook's Pantry

Minced Onion, Minced Ginger & Minced Garlic

This little trick saves time, it saves washing up extra utensils with every meal, and it's so easy!! You'll need to buy small containers with lids, which are available in various sizes in Asian supermarkets.

Method

Onions:

Peel the onions, chop into large pieces and process in a small food processor.

Using a teaspoon, place minced onion into containers (1/2 cup capacity). Cover tightly with lid and freeze for up to 2 weeks. Alternatively, you can pour a little olive oil over the top of the minced onion, cover tightly with lid and refrigerate for up to 3 days.

Ginger:

Peel the ginger, chop into small pieces and process in a small food processor.

Using a teaspoon, place small amounts of the ginger into smaller containers (30 - 40mls capacity). Cover tightly with lid and freeze for up to 1 month.

Garlic:

Peel the garlic and process in a small food processor.

Using a teaspoon, place small amounts of the garlic into smaller containers (30 - 40mls capacity). Cover tightly with lid and freeze for up to 1 month.

 **CHOOK'S TIPS**

Buy these ingredients in larger quantities. It's cost effective and saves you hours of cooking time.

Béchamel (White) Sauce

If you can master the white sauce, you've just added many more tasty recipes to your culinary repertoire. It's not as scary as you may think. Practice, as with everything, is the key, although with the following steps, you're bound to perfect it in no time.

Ingredients – makes approximately 1½ cups

50g butter
50g plain flour
300ml milk

Method

Place the butter in a small saucepan over a low heat. When butter has just melted, add the flour all at once, stir to combine with a wooden spoon and cook over the heat for approximately 1 minute. This is called the roux. At this stage, the roux can be cooled completely and rolled into golf ball size pieces, wrapped individually in cling film and frozen for later use to thicken soups and casseroles or gravy.

To make a white sauce, remove saucepan away from the heat. Add the milk to the roux, a little at a time, and stir well to thoroughly combine at each addition. This will ensure a lump free consistency. When all the milk has been added and your paste is smooth, return the saucepan to a low heat and cook the sauce, stirring constantly until it thickens. Add salt and pepper to season. Add grated cheese to make a Mornay sauce.

 CHOOK'S TIPS

I love Béchamel sauce, especially when cheese is added for a great lobster Mornay. Flavour variations for your Béchamel: Add an egg yolk to enrich your sauce or use half milk and half chicken stock for a really full bodied flavour. Other white sauce recipe suggestions: chicken and leek pie, fish pie, lasagne, soufflé, or as a thickener for soups and casseroles, and a good old macaroni and cheese bake.

About the author

Monique is an author, entrepreneur, public speaker and voice over artist.

Monique has worked most of her life in hospitality, promotions and customer service, and later providing professional staff to many corporations for product launches, exhibitions, and trade events. When she opened her own promotional agency, Australia in Style, she soon became one of the most in demand promotional agents in Australia.

After years of success, the economy took a turn and the business failed. Determined to restore her success, and with the help of her sister, Monique created another promotional modelling agency called Vanity the Agency.

With this new business, she began a 15-year-long effort to change people's negative perceptions of promotional models. While supplying models for the motor show niche, she found herself in the position of fulfilling requests for a very narrow type of model. Through the power of persuasion, Monique was able to broaden the type of models who worked these events, eliminating height restrictions and including people of all ethnicities, males as well as females and plus size models. She was also responsible for many teams being dressed in comfortable, stylish outfits.

Soon after the global financial crisis hit in 2009, motor shows ceased in Australia. Monique reinvented herself by opening her house to foreign students, where she became a house mother to many international teens. (And they were great taste testers for the recipes). She found this role extremely rewarding because she was able to teach young people to speak English, how to cook and show them the beauty of Australia, whilst concurrently running the agency.

Monique has worked with many organisations including Holden, Subaru, Mercedes Benz, Ferrari, Maserati, BMW, Jaguar, Volvo, Land Rover, Alfa Romeo, Fiat, Saab, Harley Davidson, Hewlett Packard, Shell, NRL, AFL, Cricket Australia, Nokia, Samsung, Apple, Coca Cola, Radio 2MMM, Chanel 9, Nestle, Fosters, Sydney Olympics, and many more.

Inspiration for the *Bacon & Eggs* cookbook came from touring with staff to interstate events. Monique ensured her A-team had a hearty breakfast before taking on 12 hour days for weeks at a time. Bacon and eggs was the preferred meal, although Monique wanted to make the meals a little fancier than the standard presentation. When she looked for a Bacon & Eggs cookbook to give her inspiration, there wasn't anything in the market. This void led to 10 years of recipe writing and photography for the book.

Having travelled abroad to France, Hong Kong, Italy, Israel, England and Greece, with an inquisitive palate, has enabled Monique to confidently dabble in other international cuisines.

Born and raised in Sydney, enthusiasm for cooking came at an early age. In the kitchens of doting Eastern European grandmothers, Monique graduated from curious spectator, potato peeler and cake mixer, to preparing three course meals for the family, all under loving watchful eyes.

Having co-managed a busy Darlinghurst café, as well as working in a family owned café in Double Bay, Monique knows her way around a kitchen.

Monique is the author of *Bacon & Eggs* and is currently residing in Sydney. She is working on a number of themed and exciting new cookbooks.

www.ingramcontent.com/pod-product-compliance
Lightning Source LLC
Chambersburg PA
CBHW041140170426
43200CB00021B/2984